C000018357

THE SOUTH WEST COAST PATH

An Illustrated History

'A walk of a thousand miles begins with but a single step'

Text by Philip Carter

Compiled and Edited by

The South West Coast Path Association

Published by Halsgrove

in association with

The South West Coast Path Association

First published in Great Britain in 2005

British Library Cataloguing-in-Publication Data
A CIP record for this title is available from the British Library

ISBN 1 84114 489 4

THE SOUTH WEST COAST PATH ASSOCIATION
Windlestraw
Penquit
Ermington
Devon PL21 0LU
England
Tel/fax: 01752 896237
email: info@swcp.org.uk
website: www.swcp.org.uk

HALSGROVE
Halsgrove House
Lower Moor Way
Tiverton, Devon EX16 6SS
Tel: 01884 243242
Fax: 01884 243325
email: sales@halsgrove.com
website: www.halsgrove.com

Printed and bound in Great Britain by CPI Bath

Foreword

When some years ago I suggested that a history of the South West Coast Path Association was much needed, I appreciated that Philip Carter was the one person uniquely qualified to write it and I am delighted that he has now taken up the challenge.

The story starts with the origins of the path – had we really remembered that it was essential for the coastguards to see into every cove and inlet – and then quickly moves on to the creation of the Association in 1973 following the disquiet of the Carter family and others, at the condition of the coastal route. Were those modest aspirations too much to hope for; a complete and continuous path, on the coast, well maintained and waymarked? What dedication and enthusiasm was needed to embark on this project!

We are taken through the development and growth of the Association and its struggle to achieve its aims and, refreshingly, the author pulls no punches when detailing their continuing problems and difficulties with the Countryside Commission (now Agency), County Councils, local authorities and the Exmoor National Park and their reaction to suggestions from a mere path user.

However attitudes and perceptions have changed over the years, the Association has grown in numbers, stature and influence, beyond the wildest dreams of those few original members and we are shown how the authorities' view of the path has changed as well. Recognised now as a valuable asset, vast improvements in the route are being achieved.

Tribute is paid to committee members and individuals who have helped the Association and in particular Eric Wallis for his tremendous work as Secretary since 1987 and Brian Panton for his years as Chairman.

We learn much about those areas where improvements have been obtained and later chapters deal with specific aspects of the Association's work – Public Enquiries, Path Descriptions etc. I particularly enjoyed the one on Newsletters with those quotes from happy walkers on completing the path.

This is an immensely readable history with amusing and interesting observations and anecdotes by Philip who knows the path so well and when you have read it you will have no doubt that we would not have the South West Coast Path, as it is today, had it not been for the Association's efforts. Thanks to this book we will not lose sight of what has gone before – it will be enjoyed by all who love our path.

Surely it is only fitting that shortly before publication, the first new section of the coast path has been opened within that infamous route from Strete Gate to Warren Point!

Frederick White

DEDICATION

To all those, named and unnamed, who have given time and effort so that others could enjoy the coast path

Contents

Acknowledgements

My thanks first to Mary, my wife, who was there at the beginning and then gave twenty-five years to the project. Thanks to the rest of my family who have gone along both mentally and physically with the coast path, some of them indeed from a young age. It was Frederick White who first suggested this book should be written. Brian Panton and Bryan Cath both checked their own eras of Chairmanship and worked on the maps. Tony Collings, Richard Manson and Bob Reid gave advice, Graham Ronan provided technical assistance and Liz Woollard did the proofreading. Last but not least, thanks to Liz and Eric Wallis who despite their other work extracted records and answered a stream of questions. More importantly it was Eric, who goaded me into finally writing the book, before, as he so charmingly put it, we all fall off our perches!

Illustration Attributions

Alex Wallis *70, 95*
Brian Panton *156, 157*
Bryan Cath *89 top*
Brian Williams *122 bottom*
Countryside Agency *43, 82*
E G Parrott *1*
Exeter University *12 top*
Eric Wallis *115 bottom, 116 bottom, 117 both, 119 both*
Gara Rock Hotel *12 bottom*
HM Customs *13 both*
Kim Parker *126*
Ken Ward *127*
Mark Richards *21, 27 both, 33 bottom, 36 bottom, 38 both, 41 top, 42, 44, 47, 52, 56 bottom, 57 middle, 59 bottom, 60, 63, 67, 76, 80, 84, 89 bottom, 92, 101 bottom, 104, 106 top, 111, 132, 133, 135 bottom, 142, 144, 146, 147*
Offa's Dyke Association *20*
Plymouth Marine Biological Association *137 bottom*
Ronald Turner *114 bottom, 116 top*
The Royal Navy *40 top*
Sue Jeffreys *16, 18, 24, 29, 36 top, 49, 57 bottom, 59 top, 61, 77, 85, 87, 103, 106 bottom, 108, 109, 112, 122 top, 130, 137 top, 139, 143*
South West Coast Path Association *94 both, 135 top*

This book has been produced by, and to raise funds for, the South West Coast Path Association which is registered as a charity.

Introduction

This is the story of the coast path in the South West of England – how it originated long ago and in more recent years the struggles of the South West Coast Path Association to obtain a path that users would wish to walk. In this latter period good records have been kept so direct quotations from old publications, minutes etc are given.

Minehead – where the South West Coast Path starts.

Chapter 1
Origins

Why there is a path

Long Distance Footpaths have different origins. Offa's Dyke Path was based on the line of Offa's Dyke. The Pennine Way was largely one man's, Tom Stephenson's, dream, turned to reality. The Ridgeway was basically an ancient trading track-way. The coastal paths, for example part of the Cleveland Way, the Pembrokeshire Coast Path and more importantly our own South West Way or South West Coast Path largely have their origins in the work of the coast-guard or preventive services.

General History

The history of smuggling goes back a very long time indeed. As long as there have been duties there have been those who would seek to evade them. The first written evidence of customs dues that can be found in Britain is as early as 743 in a charter granted by Aethebald, King of Mercia. A nationally organised Customs service cannot be said to follow immediately but nevertheless came into being a very long time ago, in the reign of King John 1199–1216.

In 1698 there was a move to increase protection around the coasts. Sloops were established in the west country at Ilfracombe, Padstow, Penzance, Fowey, Dartmouth and Weymouth as well as many places elsewhere. At the same time there was an increase in the shore-based establishments along the coast from Padstow to Portsmouth, some of the personnel receiving a £10 a year allowance to keep a horse.

Smuggling later was becoming so rife that Defoe in 1724 wrote as he travelled westwards that he was unable to 'find any foreign commerce except it be what we call smuggling and roguing, which I may say, is the reigning commerce of all this part of the English coast, from the mouth of the Thames to Land's End in Cornwall'. Lundy Island was for a while a centre of operations, and a platform for cannon was erected to prevent customs vessels from landing! An added twist to the story here is that a local Member of Parliament, one Thomas Benson, used his lease of Lundy in conjunction with his contract for transportation of felons. Instead of taking them across the oceans, he took the cheaper option of depositing them on Lundy so they could help handle smuggled goods! He was prosecuted for not fulfilling his transportation contract but successfully pleaded he had taken the convicts 'out of the country'!

Some smugglers were particularly brazen. In pursuit of seized contraband tea in October 1747 a gang of some thirty men attacked the Customs House in Poole. It is recorded that they loaded the tea on to a train of horses and triumphantly carried off the cargo, being cheered along their way as they passed through towns and villages!

In 1755 smugglers' wives were suspected of causing the death of a customs officer, one John Hurley of Branscombe, by throwing him over a cliff. The women had lit a number of signal fires on the cliffs near Seaton that Hurley was attempting to extinguish. The verdict however was accidental death, the only witnesses being the smugglers' wives and every one claimed he had fallen over.

An incident at Dartmouth in 1766 says something for the toughness of the customs service or makes you feel grateful for your present National Health Service. Some customs officers fell in with a party of forty smugglers. Well outnumbered they decided that discretion was the better part of valour and retreated. Unfortunately the gang caught one officer, he was beaten and had his shoulder dislocated in the fracas. This was wrongly set, so three weeks later a cider-press was used to break it again and then it was reset!

In 1768 at Falmouth another officer William Odgers was so badly assaulted by smugglers that he died before help could be summoned. However all these incidents occurred, believe it or not, before smuggling reached its peak. This happened towards the end of the eighteenth and the very first part of the nineteenth centuries. The reasons for this was the long series of continental wars which led the government to seek extra revenue to fund their naval and military expenditure. They increased most existing duties and added to the range of items on which duty was charged. This simply meant that the scope and profit to be made from smuggling was vastly enhanced.

Overall it has been estimated that countrywide there may have been as many as 300 vessels engaged full time in smuggling, let alone how many more part-time and other goods being brought in on regular sailing packets. Possibly too, some 20 000 people were engaged in smuggling full time.

Although it must fairly be stated that Kent and Sussex, because of the shortness of the sea passage, were generally the areas of most intense smuggling. The west country though, as some of the following snippets will confirm, had a substantial trade too. One report says that 'pedlars carried the smuggled goods into every town and village in Cornwall and Devon'.

In 1799 Humphrey Glynn a boatman of Cawsand was shot and killed by smugglers from a vessel called the *Lottery*. Cawsand had a well-deserved reputation for its part in smuggling. At one time it was estimated that 52 boats on the run to Roscoff in to the Cornish coast had come from Cawsand. The place was well known too for providing not only the boats but also the men to man them as well. (The modern Roscoff ferry from Plymouth still passes Cawsand on every trip.)

Cawsand long had a reputation for smuggling, not surprising if a 17th century report on the custom's officer was typical: 'Ancient idle fellow set on fishing, has never done any work, nor ever will'.

There are reports of folk gathering in numbers in excess of fifty with whips and loaded pistols to further the illegal trade. At Polperro it was reported 'all joined in ... women and children turned out to assist the unlawful trade'. Such large profits could be made that the smugglers could resort to bribery. At Paignton the Chief Officer released two smugglers his men had caught, but the affair was investigated and he was dismissed, it being thought that he had been paid a price for this apparent act of leniency.

Smuggling or 'free-trading' as those engaged in it preferred to call it is usually short of written evidence for obvious reasons. We know for instance that there were underground passages at Maidencombe leading from the sea via the cellars of the now demolished house at Sladnor Park, to the main road, but it cannot possibly be proved that they were used by smugglers. However there were two notorious characters who did go into print. Jack Rattenbury of Beer was one and it had certainly been reported that 'Beere gang ... was one of the most noted and vicious gangs operating in Devon'. He tells of an exciting life evading the revenue and rarely being caught. It has been suggested though that maybe he was not very successful because, on his retirement, a local landowner Lord Rolle granted him a pension of a shilling a week. A very different interpretation of this could be made if we remember that local landowners were often substantial purchasers and sometimes possibly even distributors of smuggled merchandise! As the Official History of HM Coastguard tells us, 'all classes of the community benefited ... landed proprietors, MPs, magistrates and even clergymen'. Rudyard Kipling's often quoted poem 'A Smuggler's Song' though written much later in time had at least a theme based on fact:

Them that asks no questions isn't told a lie.
Watch the wall, my darling, while the Gentlemen go by!
Five and twenty ponies
Trotting through the dark –
Brandy for the Parson,
'Baccy for the Clerk;
Laces for a lady, letters for a spy,
And watch the wall, my darling, while the Gentlemen go by!

The other smuggler to publish his story in *The Autobiography of a Cornish Smuggler* was Henry Carter, the so-called 'King of Prussia'. He was the leader of a family of six brothers and two sisters all engaged in smuggling. The family operated out of Prussia Cove, so called after their leader's nickname, and they again had the temerity to erect a battery to keep off revenue boats. It has been suggested that his story has been embellished and this may be, but you must have had some real cheek to erect a 'private enterprise' battery on the mainland. Furthermore it must be said that he converted to Methodism and retired from 'free-trading' to go into farming. There used to be a wonderful inn sign at *The King of Prussia* in Fowey: on one side it had Henry Carter and one of his brothers looking a regular pair of cut-throats in seamen's gear, on the other side they were painted respectably attired in suits 'for they were God fearing men and went to church every Sunday'!

The Coast Path

It was undoubtedly the huge scale of operations by smugglers, which brought into being the formation of HM Coastguard; it was even estimated that 50% of the spirits drunk in England at the end of the seventeenth century had evaded duty. As A G Collings has so pertinently put it, 'clearly no government could tolerate such widespread lawlessness'. A Preventive Water Guard was established in 1809 followed by a coast blockade of Kent and Sussex, 'ye guard of ye coasts', a few years later. This involved a night patrol by sailors along the shore. Parliament decided to extend the system to the whole coast of Britain and from 1822 the Coastguard Service was born. The idea was to throw a cordon round the entire coastline which required the creation of a coastal footpath to patrol and here we have the origins of so much of the coast path that we now walk. Note too that it was most important that it must be possible for the coastguards to see into every cove and inlet, 'inspect all creeks and

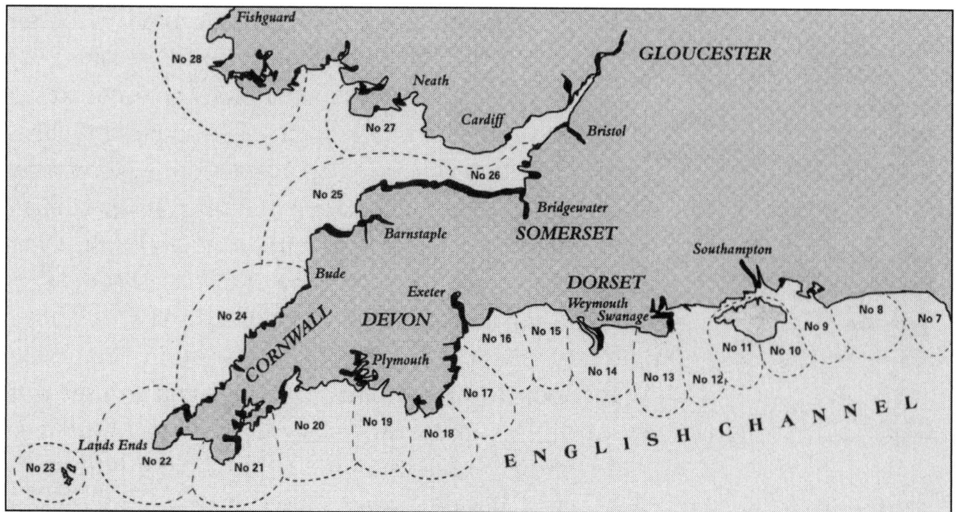

Map of Coastguard Stations 1844. These stations were really areas and each would have several coastguard rows.

Below: View of the Coastguard Cottages on the site of what was to become the Gara Rock Hotel; the picture is undated but known to be between 1847 and 1908. It has been suggested by some sources that the unpopularity of coastguards made it a necessity to build special accommodation for them. The reason for the building was much more likely to be an official attempt to lessen the likelihood of local influence upon the men.

bye-places': this meant that the path had to hug the shore at all times, regardless of any coastal properties.

The establishment along the coast depended on the nearness and approachability of foreign shores. The highest rate of staffing was in Kent with one man for every hundred yards of coast. In South Devon and Cornwall there was a man to between a quarter and half-mile. On the Bristol Channel coast, remembering the difficulties in days of sail of rounding Land's End, there was only one coastguard to every two to three miles.

To prevent collusion no man was allowed to serve within twenty miles of his birthplace, so accommodation was therefore needed. It has been suggested that because coastguards were so unpopular none would give them lodgings. More probably it was provided to lessen local influence. It was even said that local landowners had to be threatened with compulsory purchase before land could be obtained to build the coastguard rows of houses. Because the patrols were on foot the accommodation had on the whole to be half a night's march or patrol from the next. We need to remember that because most smuggling took place at night, the most important patrols were those after dark. On their patrols too along the coast the coastguards would be given messages to carry which they had to give to the next patrol so ensuring the whole area was in fact properly covered and none of it missed out.

It is because of this pedestrian basis that we still see so many of these old coastguard rows, now nearly always converted, when we walk the coast path. Some of these stations were in very lonely and isolated places, the one at Weston Mouth for instance. Here there were four cottages at the foot of the cliffs the only way down being by steep paths, as today, but then surely narrower. Shopping was obviously an expedition! and it is reported that furniture had to be lowered down the cliffs by ropes.

There were various changes over time in the organisation and administration of the service. In 1832 the coastguard became the reserve for the Royal Navy. Later, after the Crimean War in 1856, control of the whole service passed to the

A group of coastguards training at West Bay in 1864.

Admiralty, officially so that it would be better trained in future. Another version of the reason for this is that the revenue authorities thought at an early date that patrolling on foot was not effective and wished to abandon it. However the Admiralty, in the days when the British Navy was still secure in its important position as senior service and first line of defence, would have none of this so they took it over themselves. Evidence of the Admiralty's control is still around, for instance if you are in Portscatho and look at the old coastguard row you will see it is named 'Admiralty Row', you can therefore be sure it dates from the Admiralty's period of tenure.

In the Merchant Shipping Act of 1854 Customs Officers' responsibilities as 'receivers of wreck' were reiterated. Evidence of the deliberate wrecking of vessels is even more difficult to come by than that of smuggling, possibly because it was in fact rare. However there is no doubt whatever, how often and quickly folk would flock to an accidental wreck and despoil it before the goods could be legitimately secured. In fact there were occasions when officers were forced to flee for their lives in the face of determined spoilers. The name of one of the islands at Bedruthan Steps, Samaritan, reminds us of one notorious example, the wreck of *The Good Samaritan,* an East India Company ship, at Bedruthan Steps in1846. A large number of local men had cause to regret their activities in the County Jail at Bodmin. If you think the despoiling of wrecks is just history think again! *The Demetrios* that ran ashore near Prawle Point in December 1992 was plundered.

The new improved coastguard services certainly proved effective. Again to quote from Collings, 'superior training and full-time commitment of the coastguard gained the upper hand, forcing the smugglers to resort to smaller scale, more covert methods'. Thus was ushered in what some writers have dubbed as the 'scientific period' of smuggling! However there is little doubt that it was the increased introduction of free trade which really cut the ground from under the smugglers' feet. When nearly all trade was free there was little scope for illicit 'free-traders'!

As a result smuggling vastly decreased and *Punch,* the humorous magazine, even described coastguard stations as 'castles of idleness'. A charge that those involved would heartily refute but nonetheless it became more and more obvious that the once pressing need for regular patrols had long since gone. The Admiralty itself started to look hard at the Coastguard Service wondering if it was getting value for the money it was spending. Over the years various economies had been made and numbers reduced. By 1906 personnel totalled about 4000 and the future of the service became the matter of debate between the Customs Board and the Admiralty. This time it was apparently the Admiralty wishing to scale down and the Board of Customs not being so keen. However government matters proceeded slowly in those times and no real decisions had been made

Coastguards on parade at Teignmouth in 1911: this was at a late date but evidence the service was still active. Note the nautical style uniforms.

when World War I intervened in 1914 delaying still further the final outcome. However finally by 1922 the Government had time to set up a committee to examine the situation. They decided that the maintenance of a large force on the coast in peacetime could not be justified. A continuous watch over stretches of the coast was no longer necessary except at main lookout stations.

The foot patrols were therefore abandoned. There is doubt exactly when, 1913 has long been posited and some authorities have even suggested as late as 1922. Yet in the Public Record Office, Cust 69/194 there is a letter from the Collector at Ilfracombe to his superior the Collector at Bristol. This was written on 11/8/1913, in which he says:- 'many years ago when a regular coastguard patrol was in existence from Croyde to Combe Martin'. It seems probable that there was a gradual run-down; whenever it was present day coast path walkers can only wish they had continued longer. If they had there would have been a shorter period for enclosers and developers to do their worst.

Smuggling over the years has at times had for some people, a romantic aura, whereas in fact it was often a nasty, brutal business. Nonetheless we still come back to the fact that the greater part of the path we walk with so much pleasure today, has its origins in the struggles to collect duties in the heyday of smuggling. Maybe we too, for very different reasons, should see some romance in 'free-trading'!

More Modern Developments

Unfortunately the coast path never achieved throughout its length full legal status as a right of way. This despite the fact it was used by many others, not just coastguards, over the years, for instance fishermen's wives visiting the next village. There are too the records of early travellers such as Walter White who walked a lot of the path in 1854. Tony Collings reminded us of some of his local adventures. Crossing the Dart by ferry 'with its two guide chains, a lumbering machine worked by horses'. White mentions the slate quarries beyond Torcross 'where the noise of a steam engine and of machinery for squaring the slabs seem an intrusion' and so on to 'the primitive-looking fishy-smelling village of Beesands'. At Hallsands he had difficulty in getting the landlady of the *London Inn* to give him a makeshift bed of four chairs and a blanket. However, he wrote 'for a few minutes I heard the solemn plunge of the surge upon the beach, not forty feet from the window; and then – I never slept better'. Early the next day the wife of the assistant keeper at Start Point Lighthouse provided him a breakfast of coffee and mutton chops for which he agreed to deliver a letter to 'our uncle, the head keeper at the Lizard'.

Tony Collings has also written up one of the infamous law cases of the right to use the path, that of The Queen v Ames. This took three years to resolve from 1840 to 1843 but came to a happy solution. Such cases have gone a long way to determine whether we should be able to continue to enjoy what was formerly open to us, or whether access could be denied. Sadly all too often, the enjoyment of the many was to be curtailed by the acquisitiveness of the few.

During the bleak years of the Second World War thought was given by committees to various matters that might be pursued in peacetime when the war was over. One of these, the Hobhouse, discussed the setting up of National Parks and Long Distance Footpaths among other suggestions for these paths were the coastal paths of Devon and Cornwall. After the war enactment followed in the 1949 National Parks and Access to the Countryside Act.

Progress up to that stage, bearing in mind the constraints of wartime, could be said to have been rapid. What followed was a long period of exceedingly slow and it must be said strikingly inept progress. To be fair there was a new governmental agency originally the National Parks Commission, later the Countryside Commission and later still the Countryside Agency which embarked on something they had never done before. However they certainly did not help themselves by the excessive secrecy with which they tried to cloak their activities and their complete disregard of the opinions of likely users of the path for whom they were meant to be providing it. More on those points later.

Dart ferry. A much more recent picture of a 'floating bridge' ferry across the River Dart, now propelled by a diesel tug not horses. Guess what time of year it is from the decoration on board?

Chapter 2

Why our Association Began

The Conception

In 1972 Mary, my wife, and I with three of our children, Susan, Timothy and Peter had walked the Pennine Way. Peter the youngest was just eleven. Although, she was later loath to admit it, Mary had actually made the original suggestion for our walk. Be that as it may, we all voted it quite the best holiday we had ever had. There was the sense of adventure, a challenge met and overcome. There was the friendliness of both other walkers and of the folk running bed and breakfasts along the way. We kept meeting others doing the same thing. Our group not surprisingly became known as 'the family'. At the end, at Kirk Yetholm, we were disappointed it had come to an end: we felt we would have liked to do more but it was just a mundane bus and then a train home. Nonetheless we carried with us a wonderful sense of achievement.

We had already walked odd stretches of paths on the coast in Devon and Cornwall, sometimes by ourselves and sometimes with our local rambling club the Torbay Ramblers, both as day walks and Youth Hostelling weekends. We had however, not until then, visualised it as a long distance path for continuous walking like the Pennine Way we had just completed. We decided we would go and tackle a section in North Devon and received a very rude awakening!

Clovelly has been described as a village like a waterfall. It was once a considerable herring fishing port but its living comes from tourism today. It was fortunate to have been owned by the Hamlyn family who steadfastly refused to 'develop' so that its old world charm has remained.

We tried to walk from Clovelly to Hartland Quay: much of what should have been the route was unsigned and then either blocked or overgrown. As Mary put it 'we got lost and brambled, hot and sticky'. More specifically the path up from Mouth Mill had been padlocked by the Forestry Commission, a pedestrian bridge behind Windbury Head had been pulled aside, and most of the route was not on the coast at all. Thus for the first time we became aware that what was meant to be a delightful walking experience was not shaping that way and was seemingly being determinedly obstructed.

If there could be said to be a defining moment for the conception of the Association, it was being faced with that deliberately sabotaged bridge. We had recently enjoyed the Pennine Way; here close to our home was potentially a much longer and a

This is the footbridge behind Windbury Point/Head that had been deliberately sabotaged and was our 'defining moment'. Thanks to the National Trust an improved route has now been established to seawards with improved views of the coast. Windbury Head was an Iron Age fort and has a memorial to a World War II Wellington bomber that crashed here. Some of the crew had come a long way to die – there was a Canadian and a New Zealander among the crew.

very beautiful and different footpath. We wanted others to have the very real pleasure and fulfilment that we had gained on the Pennine Way. Yet unless something was done would that ever happen? We determined we ought to do something, but at that stage had little idea what.

Next there came a period of discussion with other walkers mostly in our own Torbay Ramblers asking them of their experiences in trying to walk the coastal paths. The same message kept coming back – there were good stretches that were a delight to walk but there were many others where there was no evidence of a path at all. The most meaningful conversation though was with Ernst Walter who lived near Bovey Tracey. He was a volunteer Dartmoor Warden (that was in the days before there were paid rangers) and he had set up the Devon Pathfinders to help clear inland footpaths after the neglect of the war years. He knew more about the suggested coast path than any one else we had met and famously said 'you know even if we get the proposed path finished it is not the kind of path that you or I would really want to walk'! He went on to explain that much of what was projected was not be on the coast at all.

Gestation

So this was our frustration; we had been enormously impressed with the Pennine Way, yet here in the west country was possibly a longer and scenically better path. Yet its potential value was being denied to users by failure to implement the Parliamentary Act and a completely blinkered attitude towards what walkers would want. What added to our annoyance was the fact that large parts of the Pennine Way had to be thought out and constructed from scratch. Our coast path had been a complete working path that was largely there already. We had heard the Pembrokeshire coast path was meant to be complete so why not ours?

Our first logical but completely ineffectual attempt to rectify matters was correspondence with the then Countryside Commission. It soon became most apparent that they would accept no input from us or any one else who was interested in the path's development. Perhaps the only good thing about the brusque dismissal of our approach was that it made us quickly realise that we would have to adopt a very different approach to make our voices heard. If they had been more tactful or devious in their replies we would certainly have delayed and indeed might never have embarked along the road we were to take.

A personal approach having failed, would a group enterprise be more effective? Discussion with Ernst Walter on this specific subject took place at his house, Forder Gardens, near Bovey Tracey: remember he had already set up one footpath association the Devon Pathfinders. From this meeting it was decided to try and form an association of potential users.

Honeysuckle grows in hedgerows and other places along the coast path. It is chiefly known for its sweet scent often accentuated in the evening. In old folklore it had romantic associations: if it was brought into a house a wedding was supposed to follow. So if any one has their next generation still at home and think it was time they left – it could be worth a try!

Chapter 3

We Set to Work

Where was the projected coast path?

One of the major obstacles for consideration of what to do was the absence of knowledge of where the Countryside Commission wished to establish the path. From various pieces of evidence it seemed clear that they had no intention of making a truly coastal route. However, we had no idea just how inferior their plans were. They flatly refused to divulge this information to us as individuals.

Luckily however Denis Newson and myself were members of the Holiday Fellowship (HF) who were planning a series of celebratory walks for their Diamond Jubilee. We put ourselves forward to the HF as volunteers to help with this event on the coast path and at a weekend meeting at Stratford-on-Avon were selected to organise part of it. At the request of the HF, we then did receive a set of maps of the intended path. As its return had not been requested, we unashamedly kept it! We did have one somewhat embarrassing moment later at a meeting with the Commission explaining how we knew exactly what they were trying to do!

However it was the sight of these maps showing just how often the path was to be away from the coast and the large number of gaps in it that really sharpened our resolve to do something.

Preparation

We invited a few people we knew would be interested to a meeting on Friday 1 December 1972 at our house, Beaver Lodge, in Newton Abbot. At this meeting we decided we would proceed and a further evening meeting was fixed for Friday 29 December. We called ourselves the 'Steering Committee' of The South West Peninsula Coast Path (Provisional Association). We set out from the outset to accomplish four aims and they are reproduced exactly as they appeared in our first public document.

Hasten completion of the South West Coastal Footpath.
To make the South West Coastal Footpath a continuous walk.
To keep the South West Coastal Footpath on the coast.
To provide a body of informed opinion to actively promote users' interests.

We had some early correspondence with the Ramblers' Association, and having established that they agreed with our objectives we were glad to accept advice from them and for two years monetary assistance to aid formation until we could become financially viable. We discussed the Pennine Way Council and Offa's Dyke Association which we hoped might be examples for us. The Pennine Way Council proved to be rather a different type of organisation but for the Offa's Dyke Association see below. We also happily obtained the voluntary services of Derek Hexter, a qualified accountant who worked in the charity field. He was to stay with us for twenty-five years and set us firmly on the path of financial probity.

Offa's Dyke Association

We were cognisant of the Offa's Dyke Association which appeared to be doing something similar for their path along the English-Welsh border. We corresponded and Mary and I arranged during a brief Christmas holiday in 1972 to meet Frank Noble, their founder and secretary. We remember staying in an hotel at Leominster with an enormous Christmas tree in their ballroom which had been used as the centre piece of a local children's party. The next day we went to see Frank.

Logo of the Offa's Dyke Association that performs a similar function to our own Association. Frank Noble their founder gave us advice on how to set up our coast path organisation.

He was welcoming and practical. He told us much about what the Offa's Dyke Association had done and what they hoped to achieve. However he was very much a realist. He warned us firstly how very difficult it was to influence the Countryside Commission. Secondly, I well remember him, looking straight at us, warning us that if we went ahead what a hard road we would have to travel and the enormous amount of work that it would entail. However he did say that if we wished to continue he would be glad to offer further advice and if we felt we needed it, help. We returned home that winter's day thoughtful but still intent.

Implementation

The first public meeting was fixed for Saturday afternoon 27 January 1973 at the Community Centre (now Courtenay Centre) in Newton Abbot. The idea of this public meeting was to see if we felt there would be sufficient support to justify an association. Naturally we invited people we thought might be interested such as members of local Ramblers' and Youth Hostel Associations. However we had to rely on announcements in the local press to arouse general interest.

The Agenda had Chairman's 'Introduction', Secretary's 'Explanation' and Treasurer's 'Extortion'. The Chairman explained the purpose of the meeting and gave the proposed date of the inaugural meeting to form the Association proper on the 5 May. The Secretary gave a brief account of business conducted so far. The Treasurer suggested a subscription. Comments from the floor were called for, there was a slide show and the meeting finished in typical English fashion with tea. In the early days before meetings grew too big, the Association had quite a reputation for the homemade refreshments provided, flapjack and rock buns being especial favourites. Particularly for the benefit of Committee Members coming from a distance lunch was always offered on Saturday meeting days. It is thought that these social meals helped to weld the committee into a cohesive hard working team.

There were then three further steering committee meetings; the first was on 2 February largely to discuss the results of the First Public Meeting. There was another on Saturday 10 March and a pre Second Public Meeting on Thursday 26 April. The main business conducted at these meetings was to agree a constitution, a copy of which was forwarded to the Ramblers' Association and the Charity Commissioners: this was because of the obvious advantages that would accrue if we could become registered as a charity. It was decided that the future committee would if at all possible include representation from all parts of the path; at that stage there was none for Dorset or Cornwall. We had already found our Somerset connection via Denis Newson useful; we felt we needed to speak for all areas to make the Association a success. We also hoped for an input from local government. We had contact with the Sports Council, who said we were not entitled to a grant but they would provide certain duplication facilities.

We agreed on a letterhead. We decided that membership would be open for subscription on the 5 May, which was thought to be a good thing in view of the expenditure so far. Christopher Hall, the Ramblers' Association Secretary, agreed to speak at our inaugural meeting.

Amongst many other matters that had our consideration about the path was its name. We thought the path needed a succinct memorable title. The name used was, to say the least, a mouthful 'The South West Peninsula Coastal Path'. However, when tackled on this subject with typical obfuscation, or lack of decisiveness, the Countryside Commission claimed it had not yet been able to decide on a name. We were struck by the simplicity and the ease with which it could be remembered of 'Pennine Way'. So our bid, we believe to official annoyance, was 'Sou' West Way'.

Not only did the authorities have this long-winded name but they refused to look at the path as a whole. Evidence for this is in the title of an early book *Coastal Paths of the South West.* At the start they were regarding it as six paths. They rather quaintly, or with geographical unawareness, included Mousehole and Newlyn as part of the North Cornwall Path. They did solve this later by reducing Cornwall to one path but they still talked, for instance, of Somerset and North Devon as a path on its own. This kind of thinking led to all sorts of idiosyncrasies in the ways the paths were administered, waymarked etc. As we argued then they did not talk about the Derbyshire or the Durham Path on the Pennine Way so why adopt this divisive technique here?

Keigwen is an attractive old house in Mousehole; it is reputed to be the one survivor from the time when the Spaniards set fire to the place in 1595; they went on to pillage Newlyn and Penzance as well. Mousehole has associations with Dylan Thomas. The Yglesias sisters who founded a bird sanctuary, and wrote The Cry of a Bird, *lived here.*

However despite all the doubts we had about what we had to do and indeed even how to set about it we did have two very visible early indications that setting up an association was the right way to go. Just the public intimation that we were going to set up an association led to two requests to meet us. One was from Devon County Council including their Mr Williamson, and the other from the Countryside Commission, a Miss Lutgen then in charge of the Long Distance Footpaths Division. One aspect of each meeting may be worth recalling. It soon became apparent that Devon had no idea how for instance Cornwall was setting about their coast path or vice versa. It could be argued that in those days they were separate paths, but one would have expected there would have been some level of co-ordination, but apparently there was none. The Commission although they outlined some of their problems was adamant that it did not wish to define a path on a continuous basis particularly in urban areas.

We have the humorous memory of going to meet off a train one of the first official visitors whom we had not previously met. Denis Newson, who had been a civil servant himself, was able to advise us. He said that level of official would be entitled to travel first class and would be issued with a certain colour briefcase. The official was delighted to be greeted by name but we never told him how we had sorted him out from the other passengers!

Before our first meeting we had an invitation to help mark out a footpath at Scabbacombe Head near Brixham. Rumour had it that this was not really coastal and our approval was being sought as a subterfuge to getting agreement. We therefore wrote saying if it was truly coastal we would gladly help but if not, no.

CHAPTER 4

We Go Public 1973–1977

The second public meeting at which the Association was actually formed was held on the 5 May 1973. If we could have been surer of support maybe one public meeting would have sufficed. However hindsight is a wonderful thing and maybe the extra preparation time we had was an advantage. The vote to form an association was, not surprisingly, carried easily.

The first committee elected was: Chairman, Ernst Walter, Treasurer, Derek Hexter FCA, Secretary, Philip Carter, Members: Edward Bailey from Totnes, Mary Carter, Betty Gaze from Dousland, Jim Martin, Youth Hostel warden at Bellever, Pat Miller and Joan Westaway from Torquay, J Jackson of the Sports Council, Area Members: Mary Bradby and Mary Weston for Cornwall, Harry Reddaway for Dorset and Denis Newson, Somerset and North Devon.

The first proper or full, as opposed to steering committee meeting, was held on the 12 May and a number of important decisions were made. It was decided that Saturday afternoons suited all concerned for meetings and that Newton Abbot was a convenient centre. Joan Westaway was elected Vice-Chairman. Daphne Lancey was appointed as an officer to be Membership Secretary. There was some opposition to the early appointment of a paid officer but it was hoped that the Association would grow. No less than 860 letters had in fact been sent so far, and it was felt that it would be quite impossible to fulfil the task we had set ourselves without paid clerical assistance. Daphne had a most appropriate name for her house as it was 'Kynance'. She was to serve the Association for many years and we still have reason to be thankful to her now, because early papers were saved and they have provided the basis for this history. Another 'thank you' goes to Eric Wallis who later meticulously filed them.

The first working party for local but not area members was fixed for the 24 May. These working parties, usually for sending out Association literature to members, have been a feature ever since. The Association owes thanks to all those who have so willingly participated over the years. They have incidentally, although hardworking affairs, usually been light hearted as well.

Information Cards (later Leaflets)

One of the early ways we sought members was to send out Information Cards about ourselves. These contained addressed reply cards applying for membership. We aimed for membership thus:

DID YOU KNOW
There should be a coastal path all the way
From MINEHEAD in Somerset

To POOLE HARBOUR in Dorset?
Unfortunately, this is still a dream and not a reality
IF YOU LIKE WALKING ON THE COAST
Please take a card below and post it off

These were sent to a number of different types of outlet for instance accommodation addresses, Holiday Fellowship and Countrywide Holidays Association guesthouses, Libraries, Information Offices, Youth Hostels etc. The cards were all keyed with a code letter so we could analyse which gave the best response. Perhaps surprisingly, for some while the best response was from those sent to libraries. Later this postcard was developed into a small mono-colour printed leaflet, firstly two-fold, later three-fold. Later still with an even bigger print run in 2002 we had them produced in colour. They now tell what the Association does and the services offered. There is a membership application form, a map and information about the path. We now send out some 30 000 annually.

Maps

The Association decided it would try and produce maps showing where the coast path was actually available for use. The project was started at one-inch scale but later converted to metric. The idea was that the whole path would be covered by three maps No 1 being Minehead to Perranporth. No 2 Perranporth to Plymouth was issued but No 3 never was published. This is because these maps, despite the work that went into them and in contrast to much else that the Association did, were not a success. As better guidebooks became available and more of the path became usable the necessity for them vanished. The idea therefore was abandoned.

Culbone claims to be the smallest church in England with regular services. There was once a colony of lepers nearby who made a living as charcoal burners. More recently a fern gatherer, who had a pony and trap, sent those he had picked to Billingsgate. They were used, in the days before plastic parsley, to decorate fishmonger's slabs.

Diversions from Coast, – Deficiency List – Coast Path Realignment List

In late 1973 we submitted to the Countryside Commission, at their request, a list of diversions of the path from the coast that we felt should have their prior attention. In all honesty looking at this list one could become despondent at how little has been achieved over the years. Not much on this particular list has come to pass; Exmoor figured then as a black spot and still would do so now. However, much has been accomplished elsewhere.

Minehead Harbour to Hurtstone (later more often called Hurlstone) Point.
Culbone to Foreland Point.
Place Manor.
Mothecombe.
Strete and Stoke Fleming.
Chesil Beach east of Abbotsbury to Langton Herring.

Kynance Cove is a delightful place on the south-west coast of the Lizard peninsula. It is in fact so popular that the National Trust has had problems here with erosion. When the tide is out not only can you cross the back of the beach but can also walk out to Asparagus Island.

The Chesil Beach is a shingle bank, which at first adjoins the shore but later becomes free-standing enclosing the West and East Fleets, salt to brackish tidal lakes. The large building is now the Moonfleet Manor Hotel but was Fleet Manor in John Falkner's story about smuggling.

Regarding Minehead whilst we thought the whole of the path on that section was wrong what did concern us most was the utterly illogical start to the path which was immediately taken off the seafront by a devious path inland. We felt strongly then and still do so that the path should start from the end of the seafront and because it is a coastal path it should go along the coast. What added to our chagrin was the fact that there was already a definitive right of way, already there, and they had not bothered to use it. It looked as though they had some secret agenda to conceal the fact that there was a long distance path, because it was something different and longer than Exmoor. They seemed to wish to play down its existence instead of trying to exult they had the start of the longest long distance path in Britain.

Later we began to fully list all the places where the path could be improved. At first we simply called this a Deficiency List; later in the hopes of more co-operation from the authorities we adopted, as a name, Improvements List and later still Alignment Improvement List. Today it is wonderfully presented on a CD and rejoices in the title of Realignment List, a much more positive designation. We later thought to try and put these in some order of priority. The Countryside Commission seemed at first to welcome this approach but was not so happy later when such obvious blemishes as Strete Gate to Warren Point in South Devon kept being brought to their attention.

Over the years the number of 'improvements' needed has varied: at one time it was only 80. Over the years 1993–4 we made a major effort to update and make our list of deficiencies more systematic. The total then was some 116 locations but as the Secretary said only 15 were serious. All authorities received copies of the list, as did every member of the then new Steering group. There was another major review in 1997 when a special sub-committee extensively revised the List.

In 2004 we again reworked the list this time coming up with 141 locations. A good number of the oldest and most indefensible have happily been deleted but others, as we had time and increased knowledge, were added. Some of the longer stretches have been divided up into possibly more practical stretches for improvement. We are heartened now that the present South West Coast Path Team is so much more willing to listen and look at our suggestions. We do not always get what we want but at least being listened to is a great improvement on the sheer disinterestedness of the years gone by. Nonetheless some of the worst items are still on the list after over thirty years' work.

Cornish Opening

The first event that Association representatives visited in an official capacity was the opening in May of the Cornish section at Newquay. The Secretary and four committee members were in attendance. A letter was afterwards sent out to other committee members advising them what had happened. The official opener was Lord Caradon.

The members going had provided themselves with blue/black plastic badges 'Sou'West Way': the only other people with badges were the Countryside Commission whose badges were green. The inaugural walk from Watergate Bay back to Newquay took place in the morning in reasonable weather. Between 80 and 100 people took part and every walker was proffered one of our postcards soliciting membership.

Right: *Newquay, although you could be forgiven for not realizing it, has a long history. It was first known as a small fishing community. It then had mining interests dating back at least to the 16th century. In the 19th it became a trading port exporting china clay and had a shipbuilding industry. Then it became a resort and a centre for surfing.*

Below: *Watergate Bay was the impressive setting for the start of the Cornish Opening inaugural walk to Newquay in May 1973.*

Our committee members were interviewed and had a chance to put their point of view on BBC Radio and in the newspapers *West Briton* and *Guardian*, the latter's article appearing on Monday 21 May. The official opening took place in pouring rain but good humour. Tea was provided in two nearby Newquay hotels.

A telling document, called 'Notes for Walkers' was given out at the time of the Cornish opening by the Commission: it was headed 'Local Problems' and we quote from the introductory paragraph. 'At the time of going to print there were access problems on a few sections of this 268 mile path ... These problems will soon disappear, but others may arise elsewhere; so these notes will be revised at six-month intervals to take account of changing conditions.' Perhaps unsurprisingly in view of how long it took to solve some of these 'local problems' there never was another edition. The difficulties listed were Pine Haven to Port Quin, St Anthony-in-Meneage to Treath, south of Boswinger, Pentewan to Porthpean, east of Millendreath Beach, Seaton – Downderry, and St Germans Beacon to Portwrinkle. Miss Lutgen of the Countryside Commission was even more optimistic; she said that all outstanding gaps would be clear by the end of the year!

St Anthony-in-Meneage, the church is close by the creek side and there is a tradition it was founded by folk saved from a shipwreck. The church once became derelict but it has been restored. Meneage means land of the monks.

The opening took place on Saturday the 19 May. On Sunday the 20 May the Cornish Ramblers had arranged a series of walks to try and walk every open section of the coast path. Association Committee members led at least three of these.

Footpath Information Sheet (later Annual Guide)

See chapter below.

National Farmers Union

The autumn committee meeting in 1973 was significant in that we welcomed Basil Carver, the first representative of the National Farmers Union (NFU) and are pleased to say we have had representation from them ever since. When we started we felt strongly that antagonism was not the correct way to proceed.

Farmers very often worked the land we wished to walk on. If we could establish a modus vivendi both sides, those who worked and those who walked, would be happier.

Membership

Membership, by the autumn, had risen to 130, but we would try and secure more members. We thought we needed some 250 members to become viable. Needless to say we later became more ambitious. It was Joan Westaway who proposed the next and well-remembered target of a member a mile. Of that first 130 members just over half were from Devon but already 2 were from overseas. Overseas membership was something we had not anticipated at the start but it has been interesting since to see how it has grown and the widespread interest in our path. By 1982 some ten years after we had thought of forming an association membership had climbed to 500. In 1986 we attained our second target of a member a mile. It had only just passed 600 but the path was shorter then. In 1990 it grew to over 1000 and in the next year there were two members for every mile. By 1996 it had grown to over 2000. Since then membership has doubled again and the proportion of overseas membership has increased from its early 1.5% to over 3%. In 2002 the total passed 3000. Today the total membership is over 4000, a pleasing six members for every mile.

Newsletters (later SWCP News)

See chapter below.

Yapp Report

At very short notice, less than a month in fact, we were asked towards the end of 1973 if we would submit our recommendations on the facilities provided on long distance routes to a Mr Yapp who had been asked by the Countryside Commission to make a report. His brief was to consider the inauguration and operation of Long Distance footpaths. There was no time to tackle this by full committee so a sub-committee was formed and within the time given we submitted a ten page report. This contained so much of our then current thinking that the main points are all reproduced below.

'In the matter of the South West Way, any review should not lose sight of the fact that this particular Long Distance Route was originally intended to be a coast path, and every opportunity should be seized to put the route of the South West Way as near to the sea edge as is practicable.

'It must always be borne in mind that due consideration will have to be given to the provision of access and escape routes to and from the Long Distance Route.

'We believe we are the only organisation ... that has taken any steps to ascertain the actual needs of the users of the path by a practical and personal approach to users. We find there is an urgent need for an immediate and satisfactory completion of the Long Distance Route as an entire and unbroken route. Users have expressed the need for more and better signposting and waymarking, and the provision of more and better stiles and/or gates.

'A Long Distance Footpath with a gap is only a misnomer, it has lost much of its purpose. The joy of long distance walking is

A very few of the stone stiles, originally used by the coastguards, remain and a few new ones have been built. However, nowadays they are usually wood, often built to British Standards. It makes for easier access but also uniformity. Gone are the eccentricities, for instance, the stovetop stile that once intrigued walkers at Elmscott in north Devon.

the ability to be able to walk on each day. One does not wish to have to resort to public transport to get to the next section. A Long Distance Path which is not continuous is a travesty.' Two examples of existing gaps were then given; Braunton Burrows to Westward Ho! and Teignmouth to Dawlish.

'The people responsible for the implementation of the provisions of the Act are over cautious and appear to be too ready to make concessions to interested parties at the expense of the users for whose needs the Act was framed.

'It would appear landowner influences were and still are very strong at County Council level. This means that large sections of the path were routed most unsatisfactorily.' Three examples were cited: Mothecombe in Devon, Mildmay Estate, Glenthorne in Somerset, Glenthorne Estate and Langton Herring in Dorset, Strangeways Estate. Mothecombe was kind enough later to modify its opposition and provide a lovely path but the two other estates still present problems as estates do in fact elsewhere.

'We would like to stress very strongly that we do not think that it is basically the legislation which is at fault. As we see it, it is the administration and co-ordination which requires attention.' We amplified this by pointing out that the Pembrokeshire path was finished; Cornwall took longer but has largely finished whereas Devon was procrastinating. We contrasted the despatch with which motorways were constructed compared to the completion of Long Distance Paths. We also asked that our suggestions should not be seen as criticisms because our aim and intention was to be constructive.

'The routing of the South West Way poses one unique problem that calls for consideration. There is always the possibility that parts of the route may disappear due to cliff falls or landslides, and if no precedent already exists, some consideration should be given to acquiring the right to re-route the path as near to the new cliff edge as is practicable.

'We would complain bitterly that it is a fact that no local walkers' organisation was ever approached for their views at the planning stage of the South West Way. It is an incredible fact that the people who knew the path best were never even asked to pass an opinion.'

Although outside the terms of reference we asked consideration be given to the provision and operation of ferries.

We stated that we felt there was an undoubted demand for Long Distance Paths. We said the increased use of the Pennine Way and Offa's Dyke since completion proved this. However we did suggest a moratorium on new routes until the existing routes under construction were finished. (This recommendation has most obviously been ignored.).

We made comments on maintenance, and were against concrete and tarmac paths. We said that stone stiles in the long run saved money on replacement. We did not wish to see all variety of stiles eliminated but did see the advantages of standard stiles when it came to replacements. We also made the point that as local authorities then received 100% grants for all maintenance work, we felt it should be carried out with reasonable expedition.

'It should be recognised that adequate signposting and waymarking is the surest guarantee of the prevention of trespassing. And due regard should be given to the quantity and quality of signposting and waymarking.' We then continued with a particular plea for signposting in urban areas. We quoted where they had been provided in Gargrave on the Pennine Way and where they had been found to be necessary in Knighton and Monmouth on Offa's

Dyke. 'Despite all this evidence in favour of signposts, the Countryside Commission foolishly persist with their belief that they are not necessary in urban areas, when in fact they are.'

We then went on to advocate the appointment of paid wardens 'at a not lower level than that applying to National Parks'. 'We think the present level of information on Long Distance Footpaths is unsatisfactory.' We thought the Countryside Commission did not adequately advise the public of the state of preparation of various paths or 'the severity of certain paths or parts of them'. 'We are of the opinion that the importance of accurate and comprehensive information cannot be overstated.'

We went on to comment both on accommodation and car parks. 'We note that some cliff top car parking areas are also being used for overnight parking of mobile and towed caravans, and we feel that such practices should be forbidden under penalty.'

Later the Chairman and Secretary were to have a long meeting with Mr Yapp when we were able more fully to explain our views.

This is an 'urban' sign with a difference situated between the villages of Cawsand and Kingsand on Plymouth Sound. Until 1844, this was the Devon/Cornwall border; the land on both sides of the mouth of the Tamar was part of Devon. The reason for this was that in early more troubled time it was essential that both sides of an important river mouth were in the same ownership.

Nugent Report

In 1973 the Nugent Report was published on Government controlled sites, a number of these were along the path. As time has progressed one tends to forget which some of these were, for instance Penhale, Nancekuke, and Ringstead. Others such as Tregantle have been a problem for many years.

1974

Milton Mountaineers

In the spring of 1974 we were approached by the Milton Mountaineers a group of blind walkers to organise two walks for them in the west country. The Mountaineers had previously climbed both Scafell Pike and Ben Nevis. The Secretary arranged a walk on our South West Way from Torcross to East Prawle on the Saturday and our Chairman agreed to lead a walk on Dartmoor from Widecombe to Grimspound on the Sunday. An appeal was sent to our membership and local walkers to provide enough sighted walkers to provide a one-to-one guide/escort for our blind visitors. We had enough guides for the Saturday but had to enlist the additional services of some Hampshire Venture Scouts for the Sunday. Before the walk started they were skylarking about and we feared the worst. However when the walk started they were wonderful and performed their role perfectly. They did give anxiety at one point when it was discovered at lunch time on the top of Hameldown that all 14 were without packed lunches. We had to have a whip round from the other walkers, and were amazed at how much we collected, in the event the scouts did not have to starve!

Path Descriptions

See chapter below.

Dorset County Council's Request

In the summer of 1974 we had a surprising request from Dorset County Council asking if our members would volunteer to clear footpaths so as to save rates! We wrote back saying we were puzzled, because we knew that for all the work they then did on the coast path they could make a claim for 100% grant from central government. We were left wondering whether they knew!

South Devon and Dorset Opening

This most unfortunate so-called opening took place on Saturday 14 September 1974 close to Beer. We had previously sent out 'Important News' to members advising them of the event. 'We are still sorry to say that we think a number of stretches will not in fact be complete. However, we are pressing for information to try and get complete details of what the situation is likely to be by mid September.'

We next sent out a Press Release a week before the event saying 'The South Devon Coastal Path is in fact far from being finished. In spite of nearly twenty years' delay, the Countryside Commission and the local authorities have not been successful in securing a complete path which of course destroys the very essence of Long Distance Walking.' We then listed ten gaps:- Plymouth, Mothecombe, Ayrmer Cove, Slapton to Dartmouth, Kingswear to Man Sands, Paignton/Torquay, Labrador, Teignmouth/Dawlish, Dawlish Warren to Exmouth and mouth of the River Otter. 'In other words we suggest that this so-called opening is really the non-event of 1974. The Countryside Commission state that the South Devon Path is 93 miles in length. It is our considered estimate that no less than 31 miles are inoperative or unavailable.'

Lord Amory conducted the opening ceremony. The walk at the opening was from Beer Head to Branscombe Mouth. At the opening ceremony two most unwanted events took place. We were there peacefully handing out leaflets about our cause to all who would take them. There was also a party of protesters from Tyneham who mounted a noisy and unruly demonstration. Whilst we had more than a little sympathy for their cause it did mean that we obtained some poor publicity, it being reported that we were party to the demonstration which we certainly were not.

However the biggest gaffe of the day came from the platform. A major official spokesman got up and said publicly that the Commission had never yet used compulsion to obtain any of the path and had no intention of doing so. This meant that everyone then negotiating knew that they had nothing to fear and could just argue until the cows came home. In the end of course the Commission had to use compulsion but if only they had used it in a few well publicised cases early on it would have saved years of delay. The Commission did many stupid things but this public statement about not using compulsion was their very worst.

It is possible that you may think we are being harsh in our judgement on the Countryside Commission. In case you do we would remind you of the first survey the Commission conducted of the numbers of walkers on each section of the Pennine Way. They came up with the surprising result that the majority of walkers who reached Byrness, the usual penultimate stopping point, never went on to finish the walk at Kirk Yetholm. Now it is undoubtedly true that many people who attempt the walk never finish. On the other hand the further that walkers go usually the more determined they are to complete. So how did the Commission arrive at this startling conclusion? With Civil Service, but not walkers', hours in mind they set up their census points at 9.00 in the morning. By that time most walkers knowing there was a tough walk of over 26 miles had long since departed!

The inaugural walk of the South Devon and Dorset paths was from Branscombe, pictured here, to Beer. It was a misty morning so participants missed out on the splendid views. The building in the foreground, now an hotel, was a one time coastguard row.

The jumbled and tumbled landscape of Hooken Cliffs, pictured from Beer Head. The inaugural walks of the South Devon and Dorset Opening passed this way. Underneath these cliffs are some of the quarry/caves from which Beer stone was cut. It had the valuable quality that when first quarried it could easily be shaped but then hardened on exposure to the air. Exeter Cathedral and many other churches bear testimony to its grace and usefulness.

Another gaffe of the Commission was to come up with the statement that there was no proven demand for Long Distance Footpaths. Undoubtedly the multiplicity of creations over the years have decisively proved them wrong on that score. At a recent count there were about 350 in Great Britain and Northern Ireland.[1]

([1] *Long Distance Walker's Handbook* A & C Black, London)

Autumn 1974

The Association became registered as a charity. There was then a scheme by which tax could be recovered from those members who were willing to covenant a subscription for seven years. Much later from 2000 this was superseded by Gift Aid which was much more beneficial.

We started circularising all the Members of Parliament whose constituencies included parts of the path hoping they might be able to hasten progress on the path. We do know that a number were kind enough to take the matter further by writing to the Minister for the Environment. We also considered an approach to the Ombudsman and Denis Newson agreed to do the homework on the relevant Parliamentary Acts. Later the late Alan Clark MP did take our case to the Parliamentary Ombudsman but unfortunately the Countryside Commission was outside his remit. We were later to submit two particular 'gaps' in the path in Cornwall to the Local Ombudsman. These were Pentewan and Pine Haven to Port Quin. The Local Ombudsman took up the matter of Pentewan with Restormel Borough Council who shortly made an order and then retracted it. However we did finally get a path, but how much this was due to pressure from the Ombudsman we never knew.

An unusual sight once to be seen at Port Quin – a blacksmith's shop. It was erected for the filming of Joseph Conrad's Amy Foster. *Port Quin was once a much busier place than it is now; ruins of a number of the old cottages remain. There are legends of a disaster at sea but it is more likely that economic causes are to blame for the depopulation.*

There was a meeting with Alan Mattingly the then new Secretary of the Ramblers' Association in London. Amongst other matters we informed him that though we had had some success in 'achieving better maintenance, clearance, provision of stiles, signposts etc. We have not yet been successful in any case in securing additional opening or improvements in the path.'

Spring 1975

By the AGM, membership had passed our first target and reached 272. However our Treasurer, Derek Hexter, said we were not making ends meet.

He had produced our first budget for likely future expenditure and the recommendation was that subscriptions needed to be increased and this was done. We changed the short name of the Association from Sou' West Way to South West Way. Area Reports were given at this meeting and have been an agenda item ever since. After the meeting there was a slide show of the path. This was often repeated in future years often with a quiz as to where particular pictures were taken. Some of the members proved to be remarkably knowledgeable.

Openings

We attended near Foreland Point the low key opening of the Exmoor section of what we termed with justification the 'so-called Exmoor coast path'. Again we handed out literature protesting about the fact that little of the path was actually on the coast. The opening was conducted by a Dr Badowski and he was presented with an Exmoor sheep's fleece by Mr Halliday Vice-Chairman of the Exmoor National Park Committee. In a satirical Newsletter we called it the 'Golden Fleece'. Mr Halliday at that stage not only had a definitive right of way across his land closed but charged walkers for access to his estate. Our comment then:- 'it is a pity that the one stretch of the footpath in a National Park should be quite the worst'.

On a happier note the path through the army ranges at Lulworth was also opened in this year. We had previously been invited to make comments by the Commandant at Bovington, Brigadier Redgrave. The path was opened on 6 September and several members of the Committee went swiftly to walk this exciting stretch the next day on 7 September. The opening had been well publicised, especially in the Bournemouth area and a lot of people most improperly shod were trying to do the same with great difficulty!

Broadcasts

BBC Radio Plymouth whose co-producer was Chris Blount started a series of short features on the South West Way. The main speaker was the well-known Bill Best Harris and the broadcasts came out at first every Thursday morning. Your Secretary was invited to partake in a number of these. 'Bill certainly proved that the quickest way to get a section of neglected coast path cleared was to broadcast about its disgraceful state. Someone in the Cornwall Surveyor's Department must have been a regular listener.' There is a memorial seat to Bill beside the coast path overlooking Whitsand Bay.

North Devon

We were asked by Torridge District Council to help oppose a projected golf course at Abbotsham near Bideford that would have impinged on the projected coast path. Denis Newson attended for us and as we said 'we certainly do not want to adopt a dog in the manger attitude to other pastimes but when we have to fight very hard in any area to get a path at all, we do not like to see it needlessly obstructed'. This we were pleased to do and in fact the scheme was abandoned. We also successfully asked for and obtained a route over Blagdon and Upright Cliffs south of Hartland Point.

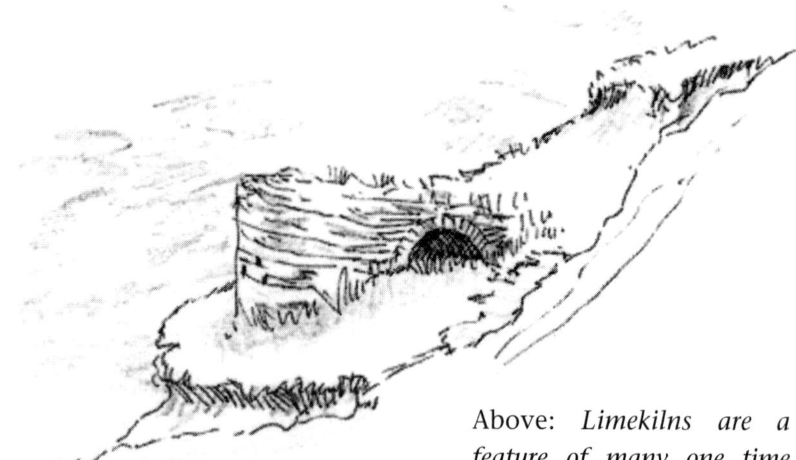

Above: *Limekilns are a feature of many one time landing places. Limestone was burnt when it was brought ashore and the resultant lime used mostly in agriculture and building. The kiln at Abbotsham was unusual in that it used local coal. A small seam ran from here to Bideford. The coastal end was hard fuel the Bideford end soft, 'Bideford Blacks' used originally to paint ships hulls, latterly for camouflage paint and mascara!*

Clematon Hill – Bigbury-on-Sea – our very first improvement

We announced with high glee that, thanks to agreement with the National Trust, the coast path would be moved off a short section of the road east of Bigbury on to the grassy headland overlooking the mouth of the River Avon. True this was not a long section, although the views are good, but the excitement was that it had been achieved at all. Well we say achieved, but whilst we waited hopefully, the local authority entirely forgot about the matter and it never came to pass until some six years later. Maybe that is a fair commentary of how unfocused any authority was on the path – an agreement had been made which would improve the path and indeed make it safer, yet nothing was done. The Countryside Commission at this juncture never seemed to co-ordinate or motivate the various local authorities into positive action.

Left: *View of Burgh Island from Clematon Hill, Bigbury, the very first improvement the Association achieved. Burgh Island had a medieval chapel to St Michael but no trace remains. More latterly it had associations with the Prince of Wales, later briefly King Edward VIII and Agatha Christie.*

Books

See chapter below.

1976

In this year we gained, although we were not to know it at the time, an important new member, Eric Wallis. He was then well known for some of his considerable walks for charity but was later to become significant in our Association. Unfortunately we also lost at short notice our first Chairman Ernst Walter. He resigned in the autumn Committee Meeting because he expected to leave the area before Christmas. As we said then 'saying goodbye, when you mean it, is always difficult, even when it comes as a complete surprise as this did. The thanks expressed by those at the meeting to the Chairman for his work will no doubt be echoed by those who were absent'. Although he was with the

Association for only some four years his role was a very significant one. He had the background that enabled us to set up an organisation from scratch and guide us in those first critical formation years. 'Only those deeply involved with the affairs of our Association can appreciate the amount of time and effort he has given. He set the style of all our publications, he vetted and checked all our Guides and descriptions. He had the most complete knowledge about footpaths of any man we have ever met. Those who have had the pleasure of walking with him will remember his wry humour and perpetual cheerfulness. "It will rain, so we will get wet!". "There's no path for the last 2½ miles but there's a very good stream!"' One of his most endearing traits was his great ability to communicate with children of all ages. As a postscript to his departure the surplus funds after the winding up of the Devon Pathfinders, which our Chairman had previously founded, were donated to our Association.

Length of the Path

We had felt for some while that a proper length of the path should be established. The Countryside Commission did offer a figure but we felt this was too small. Admittedly they did not include a number of gaps in the path but who ever could conceive of a long distance path with gaps: it makes a mockery of the concept. The task was undertaken and we reported:- 'Our thanks to Derek Hexter our Treasurer and his assistants for their great work with two adding machines and a calculator in over five hours compiling the data for us... We reckon the true path is 535 miles which is rather longer than the Countryside Commission advertise.'

In 1983 ten years after our Association started we then estimated the path had grown to 561 miles long. By 1991 we were positing a distance of 613 miles. Partly this was due to additions to the path but then some of the more seaward paths we had obtained also added to the distance. It was not until this time that the Ordnance Survey and Countryside Commission finally gave in and began to include the distance through most towns. 'The Secretary added that at last the authorities now agree that the path is as long as, if not longer, than the figure we have always said.' Even then there were errors because Plymouth was omitted and the last of the National Trail Guides started measuring from the end of Exmouth sea front rather than the ferry landing point. Our Secretary waxed philosophical:- 'For those who have completed, well done, it was further than any of us thought. For those about to set out, just regard it as being a long way to go and take each day one at a time.'

Since then the path has expanded to its present 630 miles. This is partly due to more accurate measuring systems being available but also to the happy inclusion of such stretches as Portland which were never originally envisaged. It is important to note that this total of 630 assumes, for instance, that the walker is fortunate enough to have all ferries operating. In practice, too, walkers are going to have to divert for shopping, board and lodging or camping sites; so no one who walks the whole path will get away with the minimum 630 miles!

Thurlestone

We opposed a projected diversion around the old Links Hotel at Thurlestone in South Devon. There was danger of a cliff fall and Devon County Council wished to make a longish diversion inland. It was in fact a piece of tarmac road which whilst it had become unsuitable for vehicles we thought was quite suitable to remain as a footpath. Happily the diversion was aborted and still nearly thirty years later one can still safely use the original route.

North Cliffs
The National Trust in Cornwall acceded to our request to make a path along North Cliffs between Portreath and Hell's Mouth. Up to that time the designated route was along the road whereas the unused heathland to seaward made a much more scenic and safer path.

Portreath was an extremely busy port in Cornwall's great industrial days, coal and iron coming in and copper ore going out to South Wales, were the main cargoes. Even after World War Two coal was still being unloaded where there are now maisonettes. A huge inclined plane is a reminder of the busy place Portreath used to be.

Parliamentary Committee
We submitted evidence to a House of Commons Expenditure Committee Environment sub-committee. They had called for evidence on expenditure in National Parks under the National Parks and Access to the Countryside Acts. We asked if they would also consider submissions on Long Distance Footpaths and the Clerk replied that they would be pleased to do so. We said it was our considered opinion that the provisions for expenditure for Long Distance Footpaths are being frustrated by the policies of the Countryside Commission that were never intended in the original Act of Parliament. The Committee's report was later published.

Correspondence
One of the joys of the Secretary's life has been the letters, very often of appreciation, from people who have used our guides or descriptions when walking part or indeed sometimes all the path. One of the very first came from Saltash and was from some youngsters, all aged 16, five boys and two girls who set out to camp and hostel around most of Cornwall.

We quote:- 'set off on 1 July. We camped that night at Launceston, by this time one of the girls had blisters. The next day we proceeded across Davidstow Moor for Boscastle Youth Hostel. We rolled in at about 10.15 that night! The next day was easier – we even had time for swimming on the way to Tintagel YH After Trebarwith Strand, as mentioned in the Guide the going was hard. At least one valley had slopes of about

Boscastle Harbour. The sinuous harbour mouth must have been a difficult passage in stormy seas, but it was the only natural harbour for many miles around. Boscastle once was busy, as a port, exporting local slate. These were packed in the ship's hulls sandwiched with hay. The inner harbour wall was struck by a mine in World War Two and had to be rebuilt.

60 degrees and we literally needed the fence to haul ourselves up with. By this time two of us were carrying two sacs because of our blister sufferer. We actually intended to camp at Polzeath that night but only got to Port Isaac ... It poured with rain all the way from St Buryan via Lamorna to Penzance. The path is tricky in places but not too difficult except for shoulder high bracken which made us leaking wet .... It is disappointing that there is no defined path just before Polperro – the road walk is rather boring as well as being hard on the feet. Our last camp site was at Looe and then we split up and went home our own ways. In all it was an achievement and an enjoyable break.'

Public Enquiries

See chapter below.

1977

Joan Westaway was elected Chairman in Ernst Walter's stead at the Annual General Meeting. Joan had been a founder member of the Torbay Ramblers a local walking group and worked professionally for Torquay Council. Ron Vinnicombe the long standing Chairman of Devon Ramblers was nominated and elected to the Committee. He had previously assisted John Trevelyan at the Kingswear Public Enquiry and was to become our lead in several public enquiries in future.

We were pleased that as an organisation we were getting better known. We had been mentioned in the Ramblers' Association *Rucksack* and in the Youth Hostel Association's Annual Handbook. We had also had an acknowledgement in all three volumes of the new *Letts Guides* to the coast path. We also offered an odd statistic in 1977 that never seems to have been repeated or updated; this was that to complete the path one would have to walk a million paces!

We decided to purchase for sale both metal and cloth badges. The metal badges were to fade from the scene, a commentary on 'dressing down'? but cloth badges are still a useful seller, about 125 per year in the current range of merchandise.

HMS Cambridge, Heybrook Bay

We tried to establish if there was a fixed firing pattern at the Royal Navy's gunnery school, here as at Lulworth. Unfortunately there was not. There was correspondence with the commanding officer who obviously had some wit because he wrote: 'thereby letting us continue our work in as much peace as firing guns will allow!' A diversionary path was made to be used when firing was in progress. Then, as the Irish terrorist threat increased, there were fears of a locked gate on the coast path but this was resisted both by our Association and local interests. The original diversionary path had to be re-routed to completely avoid the camp altogether. The gunnery school has more recently been closed so there is now no need for the diversion.

Coverack

We were invited to attend the opening of the new Youth Hostel at Coverack. Some of our members had been long time hostellers so found it rather strange to be offered sherry in a hostel – at least we were not asked to do a duty! We also took the opportunity of telling the man from the Countryside Commission that there was no coast path past the hotel in which he, and in

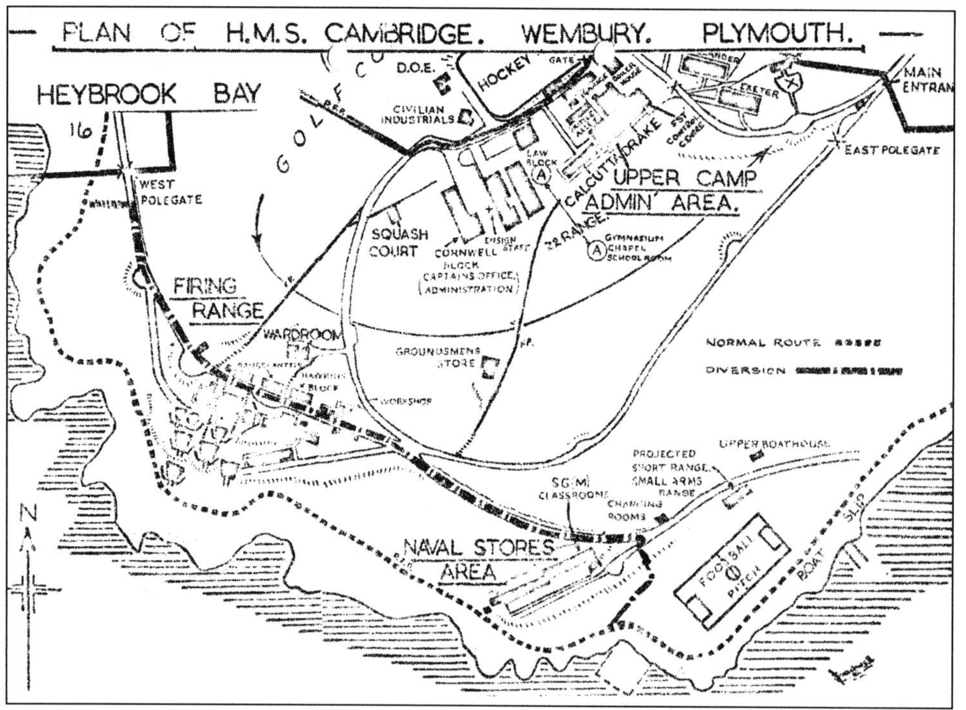

The gunnery range at HMS Cambridge could have made problems for the coast path but the Royal Navy were always most helpful in providing a route, albeit it was different when they were firing! When the sports field was laid out next to the coast path some old garden soil was obtained for levelling. This soil was brimful of Californian Poppy seed and for a brief while there was a blaze of startling and unexpected colour there.

fact the Chairman of the Commission, were staying. This particular inland diversion was a long running grievance because it passed close to a pig farm. The truly coastal path was not achieved here on Chynalls Cliff until 2003! Twenty-six years later!

Evidence

We attended at Taunton Lord Porchester's Exmoor Study. The principal concern was that more and more of Exmoor was either being cultivated or turned into grassland for grazing so that the traditional heath and heather habitat was disappearing. The study did also consider 'facilities for enjoyment of, and open air recreation in the National Park'. Alan Mattingly the Ramblers' Association National Secretary was also present.

Mouth Mill – West of Clovelly

The barbed wire obstruction on the path to Fatacott Cliff was cleared and the path signed all the way. This was significant because it was the obstructions on this stretch of path that had given rise to our Association being formed, but it had taken five long years to achieve this.

Mouth Mill relatively close to Clovelly escapes the crowds. It is reputedly the setting that inspired Charles Kingsley's The Water-Babies.

CHAPTER 5

We Become Established 1978–1988

View across the Dart from Combe Point. When we first enquired why no coastal footpath was planned here we were glibly told it was an area totally unsuitable for a coastal path! Happily then, The Women's Institute for their jubilee celebration, bought the land and gave it to the National Trust. A lesson in how ownership can affect suitability!

No one has yet worked out how many of these you hear if you walk the whole coast path!

1978

Our Chairman reported:- 'our Association was now accomplishing a more worth while role. For some while we had a lot of work without much result; now it seemed at least that our opinion was often asked, even if our suggestions were not always adopted.' We had a request for life membership of the Association; this was something else we had not anticipated. However our Treasurer, Derek Hexter, approved of the idea because it would give us additional funds so we went ahead fixing the subscription at £25. The life membership subscriptions were invested in Charifund Units so that they would continue to provide the funds to service the life members. Happily we now have close on three hundred life members. At the AGM we had an unusual apology for absence because 'the spider orchids were now out on the Dancing Ledges'.

Devon Definitive Review

We attempted to claim rights of way on six parts of the Devon coast and appealed for anyone amongst our members who had walked these to assist us. The stretches we chose were:

1. Lee Abbey Estate, Lynton
2. The old coastguard path south of the road Croyde Bay to Saunton
3. Hink's Boatyard, Appledore to the Skern, Northam Burrows Countryside Park
4. Hartland, Upright Cliff to Smoothlands there was a short gap in definitive path here.
5. Strete Gate/ Blackpool/ coast seawards of Little Dartmouth.
6. Holcombe to Dawlish.

Apart from self-congratulations on spotting trouble early there is not a lot of joy in this list. Numbers 3 and 6 have been partly achieved, number 4 completely, but the others at the time of writing are still unresolved. Later the path out to Skern achieved an unwanted distinction; it became the only known municipal rubbish dump operating in a Countryside Park. The scenes of devastation, the smell, the clouds of voracious seagulls and the windblown plastic were hardly conducive to the image of a coast path.

Maintenance

We were about this time much concerned about maintenance on the path which to say the least of it was not satisfactory. Denis Newson reported on

Somerset/North Devon. Mary Bradby spoke of Cligga Head, Porthleven, Carbis Bay, Nanjizal, Lamorna, Kynance and Nare Head in Cornwall. All these places were trouble spots then. Lack of coordination and even knowledge about what was required was commonplace. Two adjacent stretches on the North Cornish coast just west of Marsland Mouth had been effectively cleared but finished some fifty yards apart and at varying distances from the coast! In a stretch near Hartland Point all the acorn waymarks had been fixed upside down; looking as we said 'like so many Frenchmen in berets'! The Countryside Commission haughtily informed us that they knew perfectly well which way up to fix acorns. We had photographs to prove the contrary! However shortly afterwards there was a series of meetings with the commission on maintenance where Denis Newson represented our Association.

Coast Path footbridge at Marsland Mouth

Marsland Mouth. The quiet rural border of Devon and Cornwall on the north coast is a great contrast to the busy urban border on the south coast at Plymouth. The River Tamar that forms nearly the entire border between the two counties is only four miles away. Marsland Mouth is the setting for the white witch, Lucy Passmore, in Charles Kingsley's Westward Ho!

Another problem with waymarking was to try and get some consistency. Exmoor was particularly bad in this respect. The first waymark on a particular stretch might refer to some place way out in front say Combe Martin, then the next one might just refer to say Hunter's Inn. If you knew the area you would know you were still going in the right direction but if you did not you could well be baffled. The Countryside Commission also had at one time a yen to use directional signs in local stone rather than wooden posts. Admittedly these stones had a longer life than any post but they had two enormous disadvantages. They could not so easily be seen from any distance and rapidly became completely obscured by vegetation. The other problem occurred if they needed alteration.

A further problem was trying to get across to authorities that all signs except those two right at the end of the path should be two-way. Walkers did walk in both directions and very often the line the path took varied. Already mentioned was the difficulty of getting the authorities to appreciate that urban areas definitely needed signs. They were a long time coming; for instance Ilfracombe did not provide them until 1991.

We tried to see if there was a pattern in poor maintenance that we could highlight to seek improvement. Someone suggested we should have a wooden spoon competition for the worst authority. Dorset, at that time, certainly came bottom. At Langton Hive Point it took them over five years to erect stiles and a signpost when the path was moved on to the coast there. 'Even if they did not like walkers, why let the poor farmer suffer unwitting trespass for all those years?' We discussed actually sending them a spoon but in the end just opted to despatch a letter pointing this out to their chief executive. Interestingly even the National Trust in Dorset was bad whereas in Devon and Cornwall they were usually quite the best. We put this to them, and although they never admitted it, it seems likely that the then Wessex Area did not appreciate they could get a 100% grant for the work they did on the coast path.

Even as late as 1993 it emerged that the Countryside Commission was well aware that the Dorset section of the path was the worst maintained of all the four counties, but at that stage they did not seem to be doing anything about it.

Comparing Paths

The then Secretary and his wife set out on a programme over the years to walk every Official Long Distance Footpath in the country. The comments sent after some of these walks did not always endear them to other path authorities. However by comparing standards elsewhere it did give us a good overview of what could be accomplished and therefore a fair yardstick of what might be expected on our path.

The acorn was the unfortunate choice of waymark for official Long Distance Paths such as the Pennine Way, Cleveland Way and our own coast path. We say unfortunate, because it has always been, and still is, confused with the National Trust oak leaves and acorn motif.

Acorn Waymark

Perhaps a word should be said about the unfortunate choice of an acorn as the waymark for official Long Distance Footpaths. On its own it would have made a reasonable symbol but it was of course also used by the National Trust. The scope therefore for misinterpretation was enormous. At a later stage when the Countryside Commission became friendlier they asked us our opinion of the acorn and we said we thought, because of the confusion, it ought to be changed. The Commission decided, however, that it would then cost too much to do so.

'On the Beat'

We reported on a Sergeant Wallis doing a sponsored walk for the Police Widows and Orphans Fund. He walked the whole coast path around Devon and Cornwall and the land frontiers of Devon/Dorset and Devon/Somerset. The then Chief Constable of Devon and Cornwall, Mr John Alderson, accompanied him on one stretch. He wrote a report and we sent it out with a newsletter. Just in case there is any doubt maybe we should add that Sergeant Wallis' first name was Eric, who later became our Secretary.

Holiday Fellowship

Under a heading 'holidays that are different' we advised our members of two HF holidays in April and September walking along the coast path from Minehead to Saunton. These were led by our knowledgeable and able Committee man Denis Newson.

Other and a Longer Path?

We had a very little involvement with the Two Moors Way but as we made clear this was not our path. However we were approached about its southern terminus. An original idea was that it should finish at Plymouth: later it was suggested that Bovisand might be better. We have always been of the opinion that a Long Distance Footpath should have, if possible, an urban end for the good reason that it will then be accessible by public transport. The idea of starting a path on the top of Ivinghoe Beacon as the Ridgeway does seems a nonsensical idea.

We also had an approach from West Somerset District Council to extend the path to the east of Minehead to Steart at the mouth of the River Parrett. The Secretary went to see this stretch and walk the projected extension, admittedly some of it quite attractive. However the feeling was firstly that we should concentrate on finishing the path between its present ends before considering extensions. We also had the point that Steart was not urban and had no public transport at all. Later there was another proposal to extend eastwards from Minehead as far as Bridgwater. This was certainly urban with good transport links but against that not all the path would have been on the coast and we still wanted to finish what we had. Later again there was another proposal to extend the path to Bristol.

At the other end there were suggestions that the path should be extended from South Haven Point to Poole. This had the merit of making the terminus more urban with improved transport links. Again however there were the arguments of finishing first before extending and some of our Dorset members did not think it would make an appealing route.

Hartland

We had another success in North Devon. There was then a fully manned Radar station on the cliffs just east of Barley Bay. We asked if we could not have a path seaward of their perimeter fence. After some hesitation it was decided we could and the MOD was even good enough to move the fence a little inland at one point to make more room for the path. We said then:- 'We hope some of you, when you look out at those magnificent views, will resolve to ask others to come and join us. To us, this is really what is meant by coastal walking not some of the more bizarre ideas of the Countryside Commission.'

Meadowfoot Beach, Mothecombe was the setting for filming the epilogue of the film International Velvet. *The one time schoolhouse behind the beach is now a pleasant teahouse with pictures of its former use.*

Mothecombe

Originally this had seemed one of our greatest problems: believe it or not, the reason we were told we could not have a coast path here was 'the danger of broken glass getting into racehorses' feet'! Presumably the dangers to pedestrians having to walk a long stretch of road did not count! However there was a welcome change of heart by the estate here and the Chairman and some of the Committee were invited to a preview of the intended route. They were delighted with what was offered. Our news item: 'part of this coast has been used as the location of a new film *International Velvet*; so if you are not able to walk this stretch for a while, you can go and see some of it at the pictures'.

Murrayton/Windsworth (South Cornwall)

This stretch opened in the spring of 1978: we never did quite get the two ends we thought we should, even though one of them was a definitive right of way. Having said that, it was a great improvement on the previous road walk.

Dean Quarry on The Lizard

This was a strange case: here the quarry company wanted to expand inland and move the coastal path that ran just behind the quarry further inland. Our 'crystal ball thinking' was that this might be a recurring theme, so we asked the company if we could have a seaward path whereupon we would withdraw any objection to moving the inland path. They saw the point and were quite happy with the idea. However Cornwall County Council was adamant it would not consider such a scheme. There was an enquiry and the path was duly moved further inland. A few years later just as we had predicted the same thing happened again. Needless to say we were in the very strong position of being able to say 'we told you so'. This time we got our path on the sea's edge through the quarry. It has never been beautiful but the idea has caused less trouble to all concerned.

Taw – Torridge Estuaries

A special survey was commissioned by Devon County Council on the Taw and Torridge estuaries. We suggested that part of the disused Ilfracombe to Barnstaple railway line should be utilised for the coast path. Quoting what we said then:- 'Eventually, we would hope for an extension back on the southern bank of the Taw to fill the gap. As we read the original Acts of Parliament, there should not be any gaps on a Long Distance Footpath but naturally the Countryside Commission claim otherwise.' (At that date the Barnstaple to Bideford railway line was still in operation.)

This view is along the discontinued railway line from Barnstaple to Bideford. It has become a cycle track and walkway for the coast path. The power station, since demolished, was Yelland one of four sub-generating stations, in the south-west, the others were Hayle, Plymouth and Newton Abbot. These were necessary in the days of high losses of power from long-distance overhead cables.

Somerset and North Devon Opening

The big event of 1978 undoubtedly was the Somerset and North Devon opening at Westward Ho! Pre-opening we sent out a press release listing the unfinished gaps in this section and the rest of the path. The official opener was Dennis Howell the then Minister of the Environment. Later he achieved fame as the 'Minister for Rain'! The Committee was well represented and as usual as well as issuing literature was trying to chat up various people whom we reckoned were important. One lady on the Committee who perhaps should remain nameless even managed on the inaugural walk to get the ear of the Minister himself. When closely questioned as to what they had discussed she said, 'footwear. I asked him about his Hush Puppies'!

As we had predicted the whole path was not opened but we graciously wrote:- 'may we say thank you to Devon County Council and the National Trust for all their hard work ... they have come a very long way in twelve months – thank you'. Two of our Committee appeared on local TV 'Spotlight – South West' prior to the opening and we had a write up in the *Western Morning News.*

This opening marked a turning point in our relationship with the Countryside Commission. Lord Winstanley, the new Chairman of the Commission, gave us a public vote of thanks. Thereafter we were asked to put on record where we thought there were major problems on the path and we were asked for our considered thoughts on maintenance. About this time too came on the scene, Roy Hickey, the first member of the Commission who seemed to have a genuine interest in the path. We have happy memories of his willingness to meet us on sites such as Maidencombe and Pudcombe Cove. At the latter he asked us if in our opinion it was feasible to make a path from there westwards along the coast. We said it would be difficult but possible. The path is there with little modification till this day. We did not always get our way – forging a path, like life, must be a compromise. However the new attitude from the Commission was very different from what had gone before. Up until this point it had strongly resisted listening to walkers views. It seems incredible now, that any organisation should try and provide a facility without ascertaining the likely users' views. That, however, is exactly what the Countryside Commission in those early days was hell-bent on doing.

As a footnote to the path from Pudcombe Cove it is interesting to record that the work was largely carried out by Manpower Services, an organisation set up to try and give a fresh start, through work, to those young persons who had already made a bad beginning. There was one particular marshy section that had to be filled in with countless bucket loads of gravel. It was reported that some after just one day's hard work packed the opportunity in. Others though did thrive and worked very hard indeed until the whole difficult project was finished: they then even expressed regret when the job was finally done.

First Completion

In April 1978 we particularly asked for anyone who had walked the whole path in one go to let us know. We hoped what they might have to say could be an inspiration and indeed be of help to others. The first person to respond, before the end of the year, was Fred Frost of Bristol. He had 'completed the path as a retirement "treat"'. He did it 'in 72 days with camping kit, followed the coast path from near Poole to Minehead'. The first lady who let us know she had completed the path was Mary Emerson who did it in 1981. We headlined the Newsletter piece 'The First Lady'. She walked from Poole to Minehead and took six weeks, camping. We heard afterwards that she had walked with a friend Elise Penn and that they were both final year students at Exeter University.

The Great Outdoors

This then new monthly journal carried a series of six articles on the South West Way spanning autumn 1978 and spring 1979.

1979

The Secretary at the AGM stated the fact that the Countryside Commission had been working for 30 years and had not finished the path in that time. He then made an attempt to analyse their inefficiency. Part of their problem was their inability to settle down to one job in one place. They had started work in London, moved to Cheltenham and then shifted the work to Bristol. They had had a special department for Long Distance Footpaths and then abolished it. The Civil Servant staffing led to frequent changes in personnel. This meant that seldom did we find anyone with real knowledge of the path. Furthermore as *Management Today* put it the Civil Service needed to acquire 'the most vital ability of all; getting things done'.

The refusal to ever admit they were wrong militated against their success. The Yapp report had clearly shown that many of the existing policies were wrong so it was just pigeonholed. They were continuing with policies they knew were bad such as putting paths alongside main roads and trying to take the coast path inland. They hid behind the various local authorities but failed to issue guidance on practical ways to maintain the path that meant there was no continuity of approach. The reason the path was unfinished therefore was the ineptitude of the Commission. They proclaimed there would be a leisure explosion and people would spend more time in the countryside; so why did they not do something about it?

The grimmest story from St Ives past is that of the Portreeve or Mayor who entertained the King's Provost Marshal to dinner and was taken to the scaffold afterwards! The town has since been busy both mining and fishing and supplied Madame Curie with radium.

Frederick White was a new recruit to the Committee. He was a banker and so was able to provide welcome extra financial expertise.

St. Ives from across the harbour

Evidence

We submitted evidence to Mr Himsworth who was preparing a report on the formation of Areas of Outstanding Natural Beauty. It was surprising that in those days the coast was often looked on as a convenient place to dump rubbish. We made the point too, that:- 'We thought active rubbish tips and car dumps should not be part and parcel of an AONB especially along coastal footpaths'. There was at that time a dump of old cars at Walland Cary between Buck's Mills and Clovelly. Hor Point, near St Ives in Cornwall was covenanted to the National Trust to save it becoming a council refuse tip for St Ives and Sharkham Point at Brixham was another municipal dump.

Edinburgh University was carrying out a study on Recreation in National Parks. We asked to present evidence on the aspect of Long Distance Footpaths in National Parks. The University said they would welcome this and suggested we should give our evidence in Exeter when they met Devon County Council. We quote from our Newsletter:- 'Perhaps we should add without comment that Devon County Council refused to let us attend. We will, therefore, present our evidence direct in writing.' We never did discover the reason for the refusal. We were, possibly with some justification, always insisting that a coastal path should be just that, a path on the coast. So much so in fact was this that our secretary became known in the Devon County's footpath office as 'one wet foot'.

Glenthorne

A great deal of negotiation had taken place about the so-called coast path which on part of Exmoor even went inland as far as County Gate and ran for a long while on the south side of the main A39. Mr Halliday, the owner, agreed to a permissive path through his Glenthorne estate that was an enormous improvement. We went on record:- 'This would be a good moment to put on record all the hard work of our Committee man Denis Newson, who has, more than anyone else, sought this improvement and now happily seen it brought nearly to fruition.' Unfortunately under new ownership this was later rescinded and there is still currently debate.

The path at Glenthorne used to pass through this impressive gateway. There was also a garage built in a style somewhere between a Rhenish castle and Scottish baronial! It had miniature metal steeples!

There is however one amusing memory of a site meeting here between Exmoor Rangers, our Association and the Countryside Commission. The man from the Commission was last to arrive and the waiting Rangers were being, frankly, a bit snide. They said, 'we bet he arrives in a suit with a briefcase; we wonder if he can walk the distance?' Sure enough he arrived in a very smart fawn alpaca-type suit with briefcase. However, he was a superbly fit specimen and it was suggested afterwards he played county level squash. Complete with briefcase, not only did he comfortably complete the distance but set such a pace up the biggest hill that the Rangers, to their chagrin, could not keep up with him!

Penhale

There was good news from Penhale where a coastal path had now been provided. The original idea had been for the path to go a long way inland to avoid the army training camp, a lot of it on tarmac roads. Despite the Nugent Report, Cornwall County Council procrastinated for some while wishing to put restrictions on the path. Our Association reminded them that Nugent had recommended a straightforward path without restrictions.

There was one thing that we did not like about the Penhale opening:- 'We have protested about the fact that the path has been double fenced on one section. We think that most of our members would agree that such a move should not be a precedent, apart from the sheer waste of public money involved.' Unfortunately this ugly and unnecessary eyesore was used as a precedent. As a sop to the landowners at Pentewan, practically the whole of that section was double fenced when it was opened. The same applied later to Pine

Haven to Port Quin. A local footpath warden described it thus:- 'Locally known as "Hadrian's Fence", it stretches for miles along a superb rugged headland, and clings to every turn and dip in the cliffs, making a tortuous route, fit for a Royal Marine assault course! For many miles away it is highly visible.' Eventually the protests made Cornwall realise that this was a policy only favoured by a very few and that public opinion on the matter was firmly against them. No other sections were disfigured in this way and gradually over the years the fencing has declined.

Mount Edgcumbe

Mount Edgcumbe is a Countryside Park but, surprisingly, no thought had been given to incorporating a coast path until we requested it. Mary Bradby walked this over on a windy day in autumn so we could submit evidence backing our claims.

Labrador

There was bad news from Labrador near Teignmouth. Here the path had been diverted off the original scenic seaward route defined by the Minister on to a pavement alongside the main road. A Mr Sewell in charge of the Commission's Bristol office had so often told us when we asked for improvement that it was impossible to divert from the defined route. Now here to get himself out of an impasse he immediately did just that. The Committee felt so strongly about this that a letter was written to the Chairman of the Countryside Commission.

Awkward Authority

It must sometimes seem we continue to slate authority but it is quite incredible how inflexible and difficult they could be. Here are two examples from that time. At Cleave Farm on the North Coast of Cornwall, not far from Crackington Haven the coast path was taken off the coast to go through a farmyard and then back to the coast a little distance further on. The landowner was in favour of keeping the path on the coast, so were the Cornish Ramblers and our Association, only the Countryside Commission blocked the idea. Near Maidencombe we approached Devon County Council to get the path taken off a road and put on the coast: they were helpful but Torquay Council who actually owned the land was not, they turned the idea down flat. Our comment:- 'Strange that a seaside resort should be against people walking on the coast.' Later, thanks to Roy Hickey of the Countryside Commission and the farmer, we did get an improvement at Maidencombe. Later still we got a further improvement so that the whole path was then on the coast from the Goat's Path at Watcombe to Maidencombe Beach. However when the new path was created and signposted in 1992 it was found that 'this had not been approved by the Secretary of State. And the Council was asked to reinstate the original marking. This had only partly been done, leading to considerable confusion.'

This is the so-called 'London Bridge' or 'Natural Arch' near Peaked Tor Cove at Torquay. It is a reminder of Torquay's many seaside quarries of yesteryear. More surprising Hope's Nose not far away had a gold mine in the 19th century. It never showed a profit but gold was extracted.

1980

In the spring Denis Newson our long serving Committee Member advised us that he felt he was unable to stand for election again. We said; 'Dennis, we are sorry you are going; we say thank you for what you have done!' At the AGM our Chairman Joan Westaway said she wished to put on record publicly the work done by Denis.

On the suggestion of Basil Carver we gave a small donation to the National Trust's Dart and Start Bay Appeal. We later gave other donations for instance to help the Trust to buy Black Head near St Austell in Cornwall. At the AGM it was asked if a further approach could be made for a path passing the fort at Tregantle using access to the Dartmoor Ranges as an example. The answer was no, then, and for literally twenty years after, but finally the logic of the argument won the day. One can now walk through the Tregantle Fort area when the ranges are not in use. Several members of the committee were invited to an opening walk and lunch, happily discovering how good army food is these days!

Footpath Wardens

We returned to the question of footpath wardens as they were then called. We pointed out that those stretches of the coast path that were maintained by wardens were of a far higher standard than those elsewhere. At that juncture the National Trust, Exmoor and Devon were the only organisations employing them. One of the Devon wardens Arthur Tenniswood was, perhaps surprisingly, a retired City of London banker who made a good job of looking after 110 miles of path! He later came and made a report at one of our committee meetings.

On the Treasurer's recommendation it was agreed that we alter our financial year to correspond to a calendar year. Until then we had used the year based on our official starting date. We purchased our first major item of office machinery a second hand typewriter at £40, three years later we were to go for a discounted electronic machine. A different age indeed from our modern computerised set up!

Wildlife and Countryside Bill

We expressed our opinions to the Department of the Environment on the draft Wildlife and Countryside Bill.

Broadcast

Mary Carter broadcast with Colin Caley and Brian Forbes on 'Morning Sou' West' in October. The subject was the proposed extension of the coast path between Teignmouth and Dawlish: at that time the route was mainly along the road.

At the end of the year in December we had a most unusual Committee Meeting on the bridge over the East Dart at Dartmeet! Several Committee members had been on a walk together discussing Association business matters when it suddenly occurred to us that we had the necessary quorum for a meeting. We therefore called a meeting there and then and decided a couple of outstanding matters.

1981

Departure and Arrival

Daphne Lancey our first Membership Secretary retired after 9 years' work, her last big job was the Guide for 1981. Mary Macleod also from Kingskerswell took over in her stead. Mary was later to marry and change her name to Lievesley: however not to confuse folk she kindly kept her previous name for Association business. Mary had a background in publishing that proved helpful to us. Basil Carver our first NFU representative resigned and Robert Beard from Scobbiscombe Farm near Kingston took his place.

The mouth of the Erme has been described as the least spoilt river mouth in England. The one row of buildings visible was the one-time coastguard cottages. The village of Kingston is up hill to the right. Walkers will remember their crossing here, there is no ferry, and you have to paddle across the old ford.

AGM

Roy Hickey from the Countryside Commission addressed our 1981 AGM. We said his attendance was 'an earnest of a possible better approach'. He said 'that the maintenance standards, although variable, are nowhere wholly adequate... What has been achieved is some five hundred miles plus rights of way, a quarter of which are new... You may ask why the matter is so slow... However it is a mammoth task but there is not a mammoth staff. The Commission is in the nearly unique position of being able to offer 100% grants for work done on the path. However, it still needs to convince the Councils and others that the work is worth doing ... Footpaths are, unfortunately, traditionally a very low priority with Local Government ... Money is not a sufficient key to success alone – it is to have the right people in the right places.

'The priorities of the Commission on the path as I see it are; 1) complete the path. That means such gaps as Pine Haven to Port Quin and Kingswear to Man Sands. 2) To fill the gaps, such as the Taw-Torridge Estuary and Dawlish to Teignmouth. 3) Using realistic opportunities to improve the path such as at Mothecombe, Little Dartmouth – Strete, Berrynarbour etc.

'Relations between South West Way Association and the Countryside Commission had in the past been pretty disastrous. There were faults on both sides. The Guide produced by the South West Way Association was excellent and the Countryside Commission appreciated the backing at Public Enquiries because the Association was representative of those who walked the path and their opinions did carry weight at such

Looking over Man Sands to the coast beyond. It is an oasis of peace and quiet yet so close to busy urban Torbay. The path there, now enjoyed by so many, was hard fought, indeed, to obtain. Neither the Countryside Commission nor Devon County Council wanted a coastal path here.

Enquiries. Local Authorities often resent suggestions but nonetheless they should be made.

'Finally, the Countryside Commission and South West Way Association must work together. There are battles that the Commission will not win, there are battles that the Association will not win, and at times we will disagree, but we should put our differences behind us because we do have the same ends in view.'

Path Usage

It is always difficult to carry out a census of people using a Long Distance Footpath. However Devon County Council did conduct a survey for their Heritage Coast Project in East Devon. 'The surprising answer was that no less than 3000 people were using that path on the day! This may surprise you, it certainly surprises us, and to be fair it includes all sorts of people using different bits of the path for even the shortest of walks. However, it certainly is encouraging to know that so many are now beginning to make use of our priceless asset The South West Way.' Later there were to be more ambitious censuses but the numbers kept increasing. Now it is appreciated that the coast path is one of the top tourist attractions in the west country.

Cornwall – Supervisors

Cornwall County Council appointed supervisors to improve the maintenance of the coast path. Everyone else including the Countryside Commission thought they ought to call them wardens, so their function might be better understood, but Cornwall was adamant. The main thing was that path standards did improve and Cornwall's incredible choice of job name was later quietly dropped!

A Cornish family who 'made good' in London and gave their name to Praed Street outside Paddington Station have a monument inside Lelant church. The gateposts to the churchyard are made of foundry slag, reminding us of Hayle's great days as an industrial town.

Duckpool – a Bridge

After some years of grumbling we at last managed to get a bridge at Duckpool in the Coombe Valley north of Bude. Admittedly in a dry summer none was needed as one could easily cross the boulders at the mouth of the stream. In winter or after heavy rain it was a very different matter. In fact this bridge had an exciting life. Rain in December 1997 washed the bridge down to the beach. In January 1998 it was turned on its side and washed a little way downstream. A concrete base was scheduled that hopefully would make the bridge more secure.

At Port William near Tintagel we asked for and later got an improved route, in place of the original circuitous inland path. There was also an improvement at Berry Head near Brixham, where the path was routed along some road and through a busy car park when there was plenty of scope for a path seaward on publicly owned land.

The Hayle-Lelant Ferry reopened for a brief spell but regretfully this enterprise did not last very long.

1982

Spring Committee Meeting

Committee meetings in the early days had usually been held at Beaver Lodge in Newton Abbot. However Robert Beard, our NFU member, kindly invited us to his home at Scobbiscombe Farm for the meeting in March 1982. He suggested this might be combined with an early walk along the coastline there, an invitation we accepted. Unfortunately it turned out to be a morning of torrential rain. Perhaps pride was at stake, neither walkers nor farmer liked to suggest we call off the walk so we all went and we all got very wet indeed!

The Long Distance Walkers' Association gave us a donation of £100, a generous sum extremely welcome in our early days.

Evidence

Holiday Which produced an article on 'Famous Footpaths'; we were asked to provide information for this and did so. Dyfed County Council National Park Department was engaged on a special study of Long Distance Routes with special reference to the Pembrokeshire Coast Path. They asked us our views and we gladly supplied them.

French Lieutenant's Woman

Much of this was filmed in the Lyme Regis area, some actually in the Undercliff through which passes the coast path. The scenes supposedly outside Exeter station were in fact filmed in Kingswear and there were also shots of Dartmouth Castle.

Lyme Regis has had a long and at times turbulent history. It has been dependent on its artificial harbour created by the Cobb at least since the medieval period. It endured a long siege in the Civil War. The Duke of Monmouth landed here to start his unsuccessful rebellion. Jane Austen visited and wrote about it. It endured a serious fire early in the Victorian period. It was a centre for RAF Air Sea rescue in the Second World War and more recently was a setting for the film The French Lieutenant's Woman.

Cambrian Way

It was announced that the proposed Cambrian Way would not become an Official Long Distance Footpath. 'We are told that one of the reasons for calling off the project is the danger of over use and therefore erosion. Haven't they got this wrong? Surely the reason that a Long Distance Path gets over used must be because there are not enough of them?

'The Countryside Commission was formerly on record saying that there was no proven demand for Long Distance Paths and that was why they did not wish to consider others. So we have the Alice in Wonderland situation; yesterday no paths because of no demand; today no paths because they will be over used.

'Another sad fact of the situation is that major objectors were the National Parks. National Parks were set up by the same Act of Parliament 1949 Access to the Countryside as were Long Distance Footpaths. Why therefore does dog eat dog? To the simple minded both parks and paths were set up to enable folk to enjoy their countryside more fully, by access. Now the parks are apparently doing their best to prevent this. What has gone wrong we wonder?'

North Devon

A breach had occurred in the bank of the river Torridge near Northam, this was as yet not part of the path but we hoped it would be when the Barnstaple to Westward Ho! section was complete. This became known later as the Bidna gap, an apparently simple matter which became more complicated and which turned into a long running problem.

Pentewan

The major improvement of the path this year was at Pentewan. Closing this gap had been held up for some years by new landholders who purchased the land but claimed they had no knowledge that their coastline had been designated for the coast path. They therefore tried to obstruct the path. However in the end the route was agreed. Even with this stretch opened there was a rearguard action from a man close to Pentewan who already had a right of way through his cabbage patch but did not want it to be part of the coast path. Again Cornwall deferred and suggested a longish road diversion to placate him: it took the threat of a high court action before the matter was resolved.

However it was the execution of the path at Pentewan that really was diabolical. Cornwall as ever leaning over backwards to placate landowners, spent enormous amounts of public money disfiguring the environs of the path by fencing it on both sides by a massive post system chain link fence and in places barbed wire. Our comment then was 'looking at some of it, with its massive barbed wire entanglements, its miles of fencing, its imperious disclaimer notices one could be excused for wondering it we won the battle but lost the war!' Having spent so much money on this they then spent the absolute minimum on the path itself. 'The work on the opened section was not well done and we would have thought that with all the experience gained, lessons would have been learned; but still we have steep slopes that will turn to watercourses, unsecured signposts, steps without risers, it really is pathetic.'

We were right about one thing, we did not think the fencing would last. 'Hopefully, too, if we live long enough, when most of the panic of what pillage and rape a vibram sole may cause has been forgotten then the barbed wire will not be repaired and we can all walk freely again as we did not so long ago.

'What's good? A lot less on the road, you can see the sea nearly all the way. The country (when you can see it for the barbed wire) is surprisingly rural so close to St. Austell. Hallane Mill Beach, a pleasant spot to picnic; Black Head, a superb diversionary viewpoint on a clear day.'

Because we thought the fencing and barbed wire so unnecessary we complained to the Chairman of the Countryside Commission who replied; – 'The present highly unsatisfactory

The coast path passes just behind Hallane beach with its waterfall; however, it is well hidden by tree cover so that many miss an ideal picnic stop. A L Rowse, the Cornish historian, and literary figure lived, for many years at, Trenarren, just inland of here.

fence line and the use of barbed wire must be put right and you may be assured that this will be done'.

1983 Ten Years On

'Our Association is ten years old this year, in some ways the time has gone so quickly it hardly seems possible that we are that old. On the other hand a great deal has happened so maybe it is worthwhile to make some comparisons between 1973 and 1983. The main difference has been the enormous growth in walking and therefore in use of paths.

'The literature has grown too and much improved. ... The welcome increase in reading matter available has encouraged many more walkers. ... The improvement in quality has come about because more of those who write now have actually walked the path. ... But there is still a tendency for some books to have far too much information about places miles from the path. ... Long distance path walking is a splendid way to link places geographically but one walks a path in a line, not a swathe.

'The most welcome change in the decade has been the general acknowledgement, if not quite admission, that present routing of some sections of the path can be improved. ... Ten years ago asking for improvement was considered heresy; the unconsulted users should be grateful for what they had got, after all the path must be perfect, it had been officially designated!

'Maintenance too has shown tremendous improvements. In the early days apart from some National Trust work there was little positive that could be said about maintenance anywhere. Signing tended to be done as a series of unrelated exercises at specific points apparently by road surveyors. The fact that walkers would want to use signs to walk in a continuous line never seemed to occur to those who provided them.

'Another acknowledgement in official quarters, except still in the Exmoor National Park, has been that walkers who set out on a coastal path do actually prefer it **on** the coast. To newcomers this may seem an amazingly simple issue but the amount of breath spent and words written just to try and get that simple message across have been enormous. At first our requests for a path on the coast were met with stunned disbelief.

'We have said before that on a true coastal path the sea is always with you; this might seem monotonous, but only to those who have not walked a coastal path; because what it means, is that half your view is always changing. The colours alter according to the light, the levels with the tide, the mood with the weather and the positions of the shore.

'Continuity has perhaps been our least successful area of work, the official mind still gaily talks of getting a bus from one end of a settlement to the other. ... A walker who sets out to walk a hundred miles or so may well find it irksome or even unnecessary to resort to public transport for a mile plus gap in the middle, but as the amount of public transport diminishes fast, this is less and less feasible.

'Ten years' work just to try and make it possible, to simply walk without let or hindrance; but possibly some enjoyment, along a footpath. Well it's true and our thanks to all those who have worked and walked, some sad to say no longer with us.

'It is easier now to walk the South West Way, you can walk longer stretches, more often on the coast, along a well maintained and often better routed path, with an improved guide book in your pocket, and there are more of you doing it.'

Still Ten Years On

'The things we remembered best. We have walked much in company and the fellowship and enjoyment of our companions provide the happiest memories of all. Particularly we have been fortunate in being able to introduce a number of people to fresh stretches of the South West Way. Their delight in these has increased our pleasure and made the work seem so worthwhile. ... We remember particularly the red fox loping along the Tregardock Cliff between Trebarwith and Port Isaac, the stoat which we chased off the petrified rabbit near Gorran Haven, a surprised roe deer stag, not sure which way to go; and an insomniac badger one morning on Thorncombe Beacon.

'Basking sharks circling off Cape Cornwall provide a different sort of memory; seals in several places, from the Carracks near St Ives to Soar Mill Cove on the south Devon coast. Like it or not, the seagulls' cry must be the theme music for our path but the piping of the handsome oyster-catcher is nearly as common and to us more welcome. The buzzards circling above a combe on the "Iron Coast" of Hartland and the robin cheekily sharing our crumbs one misty day at St Loy provide other happy memories.

'We like to recall some of the interesting places we have seen along our way; churches, for instance at Zennor with its mermaid and the memorial tablet to the sea captain dying in far away Manilla; St Levan with its modern carving depicting amongst other things St Levan's own badge of the hook with two fish. Absorbing hours we have spent in museums such as St Ives and Brixham learning of the not so distant days in time when fishing loomed large in the west country economy. Indeed on our path you pass such diverse sights as the site of a gold mine and an early film studio, these two incidentally not too far apart.

'However, we will finish on what to us are a few of the most colourful memories of all the flowers. There seem to be sea pinks nearly everywhere; heather on Exmoor, white bells at Pentargon, montbretia in Rocky Valley and elsewhere, cowslips at Gwithian Towans, the hottentot fig at the Lizard, pellitory-on-the-wall which we Devonians like to call drunkards at Mevagissey; foxgloves at the mouth of the Yealm and maybe most colourful of all and most surprising a great bank of Californian poppies an incredible blaze of orange between Heybrook Bay and Wembury.'

At the AGM we had a birthday cake decorated appropriately with a map of the South West Way on the top.

Ernie Kay the long time editor for the Offa's Dyke Association visited our path in 1983. As he jokingly said:- 'what do Long Distance Path Journal Editors do when they are not walking their path or editing their journals? Why they walk other Long Distance Paths of course!' Well it wasn't quite like that but having a few days spare in March, we went down to the far south-west and naturally spent some time walking sections of the coast path'. He then went on to pay us some compliments on our work, make some suggestions, and compare differences about out paths. The principal one of these being the fact that so many of their walkers want to complete the path in a single trip, it being quite possible to finish their path in a fortnight.

This is a cresset, or fire-basket, for a beacon on Thorncombe Beacon used recently for the Millennium and the Queen's Golden Jubilee. Chains of beacon fires were lit on commanding hills to warn of approaching invaders such as when the Spanish Armada was sighted. Recent archaeological digs here have found stone age remains dating back to 6,000 BC.

Zennor Church has a pretty mermaid on one of its pew ends and there is a legend of how a chorister was lured by her to the bottom of the sea! If you think that story unlikely remember Zennor is the village that reputedly built a hedge to stop the cuckoo flying away.

A Quote

'You can look at a field for five minutes but the sea forever.'

The Herzogin Cecilie *was the last trading clipper ship to be wrecked in English waters in 1936, on the Ham Stone off Soar Mill Cove. She was in Finnish ownership and carrying a cargo of grain from Australia. She was towed off, taken in to Salcombe but to no avail and found a final resting-place in Starehole Bay. The name means Duchess Cecilie.*

Cape Cornwall was once regarded as the 'Land's End' but owing to its change of status, is now a quieter place. Thanks to the H J Heinz company it was purchased and given to the National Trust. There are the remains of a small medieval chapel, St Helem's.

Montbretia, a bright orange, man made hybrid from South Africa, was brought to this country as a colourful exotic and carefully cultivated in old world gardens. It was a tougher specimen than was realised it escaped and colonised many places on the coast such as Rocky Valley near Tintagel. It is now regarded as a noxious weed!

Kingswear to Man Sands – Opening Coleton Fishacre

'There are not many perks for the footpath secretary believe it or not! Having said that I must confess that Ron Vinnicombe and myself on the 2nd of May, 1983 were sitting up on the terrace at Coleton Fishacre enjoying a ploughman's lunch followed by strawberries and cream kindly provided by the National Trust! We had both been asked to the official opening and indeed had been very pleased to accept.

'The opening was conducted by the Chairman of the Countryside Commission Mr Derek Barber who performed the deed of cutting the green ribbon with a pair of garden shears.'

The ceremony was at Higher Brownstone Farm car park and the party then walked to Pudcombe Cove and Coleton Fishacre House. A stretch of the coastal land was owned by Mr Stuart Bann 'who it should be recorded has not opposed to the coast path through his land and our thanks to him for that.

'Finally can we finish with a big thank you to all those who have worked so hard to make this very fine addition to the coastal path. We are even more grateful indeed when we remember how easily it might have come to pass that we would never have had a coastal path at all in this area.'

1984

At the AGM there was a discussion on the undercliff path at Chapman's Pool. The problem was that much of the path was unstable but the views were magnificent – someone had described it as the English equivalent of the Grand Canyon. In the end we decided not to oppose a new path on top of the cliffs but to ask that the lower path not be closed.

There was also an explanation:- 'Walkers, a definition. There sometimes seems an idea that we only regard as a walker a person who has walked the full 562 miles. This is just not so. The person who has walked the whole lot may have gone further but the number who do that is very small compared to those numbered literally in their thousands who walk a section of the path. They are all walkers to us; our Association, as we see it, is to help all walkers.'

The talk at the AGM was by Richard Butler on the Heritage Coast Project currently in East Devon and starting shortly in South Devon. It was announced about that time that an area of Heritage Coast was to be developed in Cornwall between Falmouth and Mevagissey.

Completion Certificates

We decided in the spring of 1984 to produce certificates for those people who had walked the whole path. We would have to accept their word for this because we obviously had no means of checking. It was decided they would be free to members but at a small charge to non-members.

Later in 1997 they were enlarged into a coloured picture of the dramatic Gammon Head on the south Devon coast. Sue Jeffreys painted it in water-colours for us to photocopy. In 2002 Edwin Hammond made the felicitous suggestion that they might be presented at AGMs. This idea was adopted and later one member liked this idea so much he 'unframed' his certificate, which had already been sent to him through the post, so that he could have it properly, re-presented!

Maybe a piece of cardboard is in itself, a poor reward for 630 miles but the feeling will be wonderful! The main picture is of Gammon Head perhaps the most dramatic headland on the south Devon coast.

This is our 1985 Guide cover showing the mouth of the Dart In the top picture can be seen both Dartmouth and Kingswear castles as well as St Petrox Church. The battlemented tower in the lower picture was surprisingly a water mill!

Nancekuke

The intimidating fence had been removed and a simpler one substituted. The path to seaward had been improved.

Black Head the one on the East Coast of the Lizard

The National Trust agreed to cut a true coastal path north from Black Head towards Coverack. The old designated path 'in that area was too far from the sea for any useful views. Furthermore in recent times owing to ploughing the practical route has for a long stretch completely disappeared.'

Kingswear Mill Bay Cove to Froward Point

'Another new piece of coast path has been opened between Mill Bay Cove and Newfoundland Cove on the much fought over Kingswear to Man Sands section. This is still not quite completion of this section but it is another very considerable improvement. Most of the path is on the estate owned by the late Lt Col Jones, the Falkland Islands VC and has very properly been dedicated to his memory. Those not familiar with the area will be interested to know that the little battlemented tower was in fact a mill. If anyone can tell us the reason why it was so disguised we would like to know. This new section of the path provides wonderful views of the mouth of the Dart and is indeed a very handsome addition to the coast path.'

1985

At the AGM the second Chairman, for five years, Joan Westaway said how much she had enjoyed her term of office but she now felt that is was time for her to relinquish the position of Chairman although she would wish to continue her involvement and to stand for the Committee. Finally, she mentioned the very international flavour of many of the enquiries relating to the coast path and how interesting it was to hear from the 'various people contemplating walking our path'. Philip Carter was elected Chairman and Frederick White became Secretary. Joan Westaway was elected to the committee and David Squire became the new NFU representative Robert Beard, having had to stand down for business reasons.

The retiring Secretary said, of his position, in his report:- 'after twelve years what is required of the job has also changed. Our first task a dozen years ago was to make ourselves heard, to shout loudly that users must be considered, a cosy deal between authorities and landowners was not good enough, it must be a three way agreement. Walkers could never hope to have everything their own way but their opinion should be heard. Now I believe it is generally accepted that walkers' opinions should be heard.' He finished:- 'Finally, a thank you to all the membership. A few of us having an idea, that a potential coastal path was going nowhere, slowly would achieve nothing if we could not have had the active support of hundreds more of you. The present membership is a record over 550 and it is your support that has made everything we have achieved possible.

'Lastly a brief restatement of our position a dozen years ago and still today. We want to see the whole path complete everywhere. We want it, because it is a coastal path, really to be on the coast. Those who walk should show appreciation for those who work in the countryside.'

The retiring Secretary also said; – 'may I quickly thank my wife who not always without protest has walked literally thousands of miles of our coast path through the years. Thanks to her I probably have the best knowledge of anyone alive of every teashop between Minehead and Poole.'

The new Secretary went on record that his first undertaking immediately after his retirement would be to walk the whole of the coast path, which he proceeded to do.

Sir Walter Raleigh held court at Padstow as Lord Warden of Cornwall. In the late nineteenth century thousands of Cornish emigrants sailed from here as mining declined. It was once the terminus of Southern Railway's Atlantic Coast Express from Waterloo.

Trans Cornwall Heritage Trail

A new footpath was proposed, and thankfully the original name of Trans Cornwall Heritage Trail became known as the Saints' Way. It was an unofficial long distance path from Padstow in the north coast of Cornwall to Fowey on the south coast. 'One of our Cornish committee members in possibly a humorous mood informed us that if the legend is to be believed the Saints arrived at Padstow having crossed the sea on their millstones then presumably carried them firstly by coracle and then either on the heads or round their necks across the central part of the path, then again by coracle down river to Fowey.' On a more serious note we felt that this cross Cornwall link might be useful to people who wish to make a round trip in the west. The 27 mile route was not officially opened until 1986.

Canada

A short article extolling the virtue of hiking on the South West Way appeared in Canadian regional newspapers such as the *Vancouver Sun* and *Montreal Gazette.* These brought in nearly one hundred enquiries.

Torridge Bridge, Bideford

Ron Vinnicombe reported on the new high level bridge at Bideford. Although we had previously been told that there would be access for pedestrians this proved in fact not to be the case. This misinformation had prevented us from taking up the matter earlier but it was felt we could do little about it now. Perhaps this failure did later lead to the estuarine path down to Bideford and back.

Teignmouth has had the misfortune to be attacked from the sea twice by the French and several times from the air by the Germans. It is still very much a working port exporting the local ball-clay from the nearby Bovey Basin.

Teignmouth to Dawlish

The path between Smugglers Lane, Holcombe and Dawlish was in operation in 1985 and being fair it was a great improvement over the previous walk along the A379 main road. Roy Hickey arranged for a deputation from the Countryside Commission to come and look at the potential path. Unfortunately they went for the very minimum walking route which was agreed so there was no public enquiry. This meant that we had no chance to air our maximum scheme and let an inspector arbitrate.

The old coastguard path had taken off Smugglers Lane past two principal houses and kept on the coast without coming up to the road. It also went in front of a house at the Dawlish end. One of the houses at Holcombe at that time was a Countrywide Holiday Association guesthouse that provided walking holidays. The other was a private house that had built a summerhouse beyond the old path. The owner protested his privacy would be invaded. The Commission agreed with him and so opted for a route that involved two crossings of the busy main road. The owner sold out within six months and walkers still have to cross an increasingly busy road many years on.

1986

Spring Committee Meeting

There were two late withdrawals from the meeting on 1st of March owing to the weather. Jim Martin from Bellever and David Squire from Salcombe both telephoned to say they could not attend because of severe snow conditions.

There was an important new recruit to the Committee, at the AGM – Eric Wallis. We also lost one of our original long-standing members Mary Bradby from Cornwall whose work was taking her to Cambridge. There was a discussion on the caravans at Beesands. The Secretary gave a slide show and talk saying that since he had now walked the whole path:- 'At least the problems of the Taw and Torridge estuaries, the fencing at Pentewan and the beauty of Golden Gap are no longer total mysteries to me.'

Something New – a Maintenance Meeting in Cornwall

Near Bodmin:- 'Staff from the National Trust, the Countryside Commission and Cornwall County Council met to exchange notes on how to manage the footpath and to discuss how public enjoyment of it could be increased. The fourteen National Trust wardens, who look after more than 100 miles of Trust-owned coastline in Cornwall, joined seven public rights of way officers and coast path officers employed by Cornwall County Council, in a stimulating debate. We had supplied the Cornwall County Council with our views for this meeting and hope that improvements on the path will follow.'

Rugged Coast Path

In 1986 we saw the opening of the so-called Rugged Coast Path from North Hill, Minehead towards Hurlestone Point. The National Trust in this area, in contrast to their policy nearly everywhere else, initially opposed this stretch of coastal path. We have no doubt that anyone who has now walked both paths will prefer the seaward one. It has much better views and the dull inland track is poor. To this day we are still arguing it should become the official coast path but unfortunately it is the Exmoor National Park that has been reluctant to agree. One might have assumed that an Official Long Distance Path in a National Park would be a shining example of what could be done. Unfortunately this is not the case – the coast path is worse, in Exmoor, because of its low percentage of path actually on the coast than in any other authority area. Possibly Exmoor's problem is not just of dislike of coastal paths but parochialism. The Two Moors Way long distance path also had more trouble over its route in the Exmoor National Park than anywhere else, and remember that path went through a good stretch of the Dartmoor National Park as well.

Inland Coast Path, Dorset

Obviously a misnomer, how can you have an inland coast path? However for some obscure reason someone dreamt this idea up. Neither the Chairman nor Secretary of our Association had walked it so choosing a fine day they covered the 18 miles from West Bexington to Osmington Mills with the idea that the next Guide would have details of the route.

Previously when we had a complaint from the Countryside Commission of how expensive they found the coast path we suggested they should delete this inland section and save expense. They seemed somewhat taken aback by this so possibly the original zany idea came from them.

1987

At the AGM Eric Wallis became the new Secretary. Frederick White having resigned as Secretary stood for the Committee and was duly elected. Two other new Committee members were Brian Panton from Dorset and Andrew Bristow from Somerset.

Barnstaple to Bideford

We were pleased to report the opening the new Taw/Torridge footpath and cycleway. This closed one of the major gaps in the path and one originally that

Bideford was an important port in time past trading extensively with North America. It is still a port exporting clay. The bridge probably dates back to the fifteenth century but has been repaired several times and widened. In the left had side of the picture can be seen the masts of the restored schooner Kathleen & May.

the Countryside Commission had no intention of filling! William Waldegrave MP performed the opening ceremony at Instow Station and an inaugural walk followed to Bideford. Frederick White and Ron Vinnicombe had represented the Association at the ceremony. Fred reported that there was concern by both the Ramblers' Association and ourselves at claims in their publicity literature by the Countryside Commission that they had completed the path. 'Although we did not wish to be publicly critical bearing in mind the splendid achievement of the new path. We were of course concerned that the "powers that be" would rest on their laurels ... and ignore the remaining gaps.'

Windbury Head

West of Clovelly the National Trust at Windbury Head has magnificently executed a new scenic route suggested by our Association. It was the initial disappointment that there was not a route at all behind the Head that sparked our Association into life. Now the area boasts a path far exceeding our earliest wildest dreams.

Pentire Point

Pentire Point provides one of the most impressive viewpoints on the whole of the coast path and that is certainly saying something. The reason for this is its

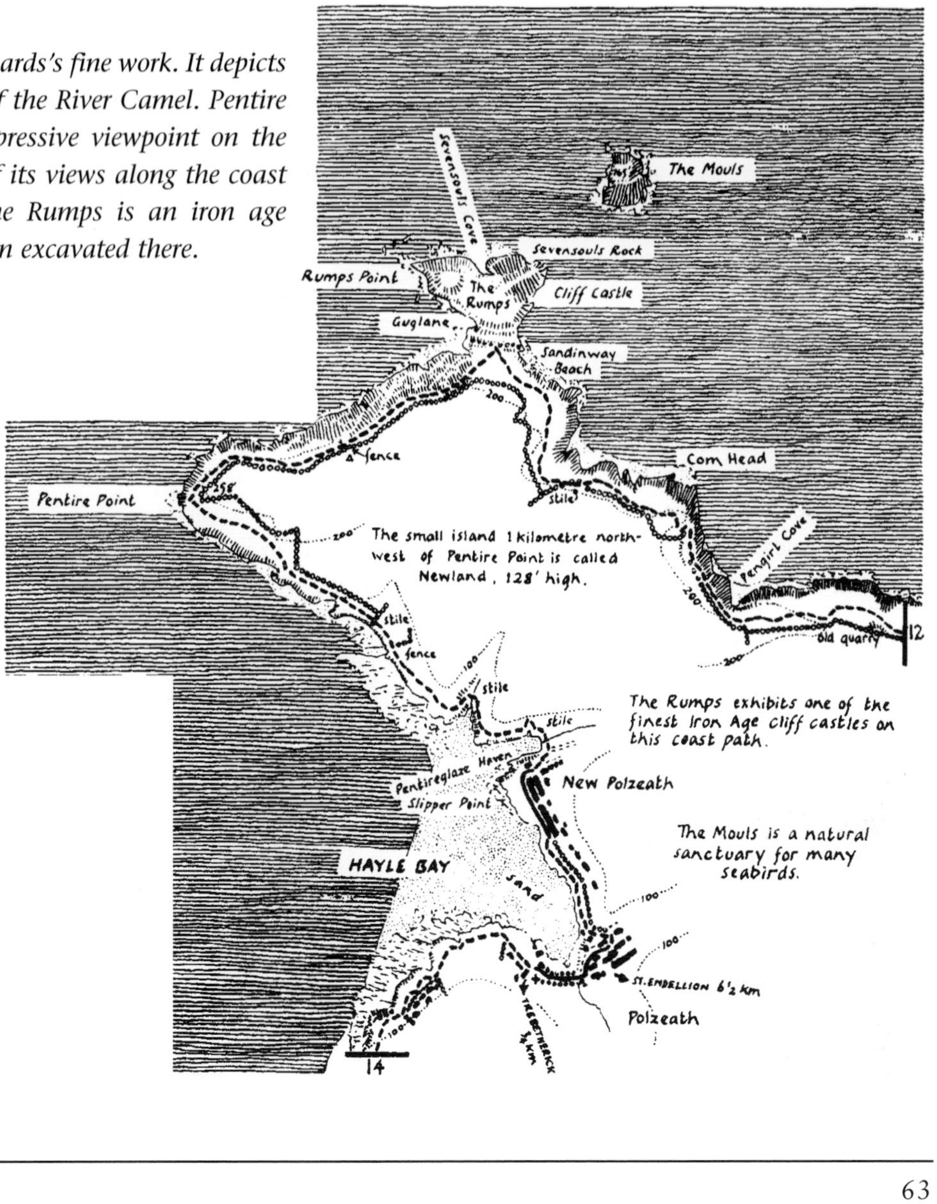

This map is typical of Mark Richards's fine work. It depicts the western side of the mouth of the River Camel. Pentire Point is arguably the most impressive viewpoint on the whole Cornish Coast because of its views along the coast and up the Camel estuary. The Rumps is an iron age promontory fort, pottery has been excavated there.

position as a high point at the mouth of the River Camel providing a 365-degree view. The National Trust had a celebration there in 1986 of its acquisition 50 years before. Thanks to the efforts of local people it was saved from being sold as development land. At the time the National Trust launched the first in a series of informative booklets about their properties on the Cornish coast.

Voting with their feet

At St Illickswell Gug (delightful name that!) east of Port Gaverne, it was realised by Cornwall County Council that the official route had been abandoned by walkers in favour of a route closer to the sea. In order to regularise the situation the County Council has made an order diverting the path to the one nearer the sea. Not only was this a splendid justification of our long-term policy but was also the forerunner of what in later definitions would be known as the 'walked route'.

Start/Finish Markers

Following several letters from walkers it was in 1987 that we first applied to the Countryside Commission to provide special markers at each end of the path. Exmoor with their usual insularity said at the beginning the coast path was 35 miles long because that was the length in the National Park! They just ignored the hundreds of miles beyond their boundary. The Commission on this particular point was more welcoming even saying they thought it an excellent idea but typically they did nothing.

In 1997 a member who wished to remain anonymous gave us some £600, to represent £1 for every mile of path. He said he would like it to be used for something practical and not day-to-day funding. One of his ideas was a start/finish marker; we said further enquiries would be made into the idea.

These ideas have had a happy outcome – see Silver Jubilee below.

1988

Mary Weston from Penryn our other long-standing Cornish representative retired from the committee after 15 years' service. She went on to become amongst other things Chairman of Cornish Ramblers. Gareth Critchley was elected in her stead. The Secretary reported, 'in the early days of the South West Way Association we believed little was being done ... to what had the promise of a very fine footpath. Our Association began to suggest improvements, make recommendations, complain about waymarking and maintenance and generally urge the various authorities along. In recent years it has improved greatly. The more seaward routes have been implemented, standards of waymarking and maintenance have all been improved. We believe that we have been responsible for several of these enormous improvements that have been effected since our inception. ... This does not mean that everything is perfect. There is still a lot to do ... and I also believe that the authorities now regard us as an Association of responsible and well-informed members.'

The Tarka Project

The talk at the AGM was by Dr Graham Wills on the Tarka Project. This was planned by Devon County Council as a long distance walking, and in part cycling, route. The idea was to cover the country featured in Henry Williamson's well-known and much loved nature classic *Tarka the Otter.* As well as the course of the rivers Taw and Torridge it was to include some 53 miles of coast path. What quite was the advantage of having two footpaths on the same route was not clear.

Agricultural Policy

This was the first year that we discussed the changing agricultural policy regarding arable land. When our Association had started the great necessity was to keep every square yard of land in cultivation. We were told we could not have a path in various places because it would reduce yields. Now apparently it was thought there was a surplus of agricultural land, set aside areas were being discussed. It might have been thought therefore that the chance to make a few more footpaths would help matters. We soon found out that that was too simple an idea.

There is probably no need to explain that this signpost at Woody Bay is not official. It has however brought a smile to the face of many a passing walker! At the turn of the twentieth century a pier was built at Woody Bay and Bristol Channel steamers called. There were development plans but the promoter was accused of embezzlement and had some years to review his scheme in prison!

Woody Bay

We had been agitating for some years that the path onwards from Woody Bay should go on the lower path which was already a right of way, rather than on the old road above, that involved more climbing and was further from the coast. As in so many cases of this sort there was obviously no reason why the better route should not be used but there was reluctance by the authorities to change it. However in 1988 they finally moved the path making a vast improvement and anyone who has walked that stretch can readily confirm it is one of the best stretches in Exmoor. Our Association wrote to the County Council to congratulate them.

Kingswear Castle

We had approached the Landmark Trust, saying we had already written to the previous owner Sir Frederick Bennet, requesting them to consider a coastal path through their grounds. They replied:- 'that it had already occurred to the Landmark Trust that the coast path would benefit from being re-routed in the vicinity of the Castle, and it was their hope that they would be able to effect some improvement in the existing route'. Unfortunately despite several reminders we are still waiting.

Lyme Regis Golf Course

Unfortunately owing to an unstable cliff and natural slippage, problems were still occurring in this area. Despite a lot of effort and in truth a lot of money being spent, difficulties have continued until the present time. One of the matters that exercised us early on was Dorset County Council's unwillingness to make the shortest diversion possible. The County Council wanted to go for a longer diversion to avoid walking through a farm that had an existing right of way.

Portland

We had said from early on that we thought Portland should not have been excluded from the coast path. However, our first approach to the Countryside Commission was turned down in short order. 'I note your comment about the Isle of Portland. As you know the Commission has not been convinced about the idea over the years.' However we persisted and by 1988 the idea seemed to have some possibility of success. Dorset County Council was considering the idea that Portland might become part of its Heritage Coast and if it did, incorporating a new stretch of coast path, which would lengthen the South West Way. In 1995 we were confident enough to put a write up in our Annual Guide. 'Although not official we have devised a route. It will be interesting to see whether the authorities select our chosen route.' Furthermore we discovered that the members and officers of Weymouth and Portland Borough Council became very interested in the idea. It was to take a very long time indeed but eventually the Countryside Commission agreed and Portland finally became part of the path in 2003. This addition as Mr Stocker of Bridport put it would mean 'the total length will then be more than the magic figure of "1000 km"'.

Weymouth Sea Link. This picture was taken when cross channel ferries sailed regularly from Weymouth to Guernsey and Jersey. Perhaps the most exciting part of the journey for many holidaymakers was the boat train, which literally ran right through the town to get to the docks. All, save motorists in a hurry, could marvel at the train's pedestrian progress through the cobbled streets.

Chapter 6

We Come of Age 1989–1996

1989

Jim Martin the long serving Vice-Chairman resigned and Frederick White, the former Secretary was elected in his place. It was decided that committee members coming from a distance could if they wished claim expenses for most of their journey at the rate of 10p a mile. Until this time no allowance had been paid. Congratulations were offered to the Offa's Dyke Association who were celebrating their 20th anniversary and we thanked them for the inspiration that had helped us to form the South West Way Association. The Secretary's report had a slight lament:- 'I can honestly report another busy year ... The trouble is that most of my duties have been of the pen-pushing sort and not that of boots on and exploration'. He also announced that the Countryside Commission had decided to adopt transatlantic idiom 'trail' rather than the English word 'path'.

Fire Beacon Point

This improvement twixt Crackington Haven and Boscastle finally came into operation in 1989: one wonders why moving a path out on to scrub from used farmland had taken so many years of effort. We had been arguing for some while that it was perfectly possible to have a good path close to the sea. Finally it was correctly planned and executed. Again we feel sure that those who have walked it will have, if the weather was kind, revelled in it.

There was a scheme once to turn this quiet Crackington Haven into a commercial port called Port Victoria, with a railway link to Launceston. Although the necessary legislation was passed by Parliament happily it never came to fruition.

1990

Gale damage

The exceptional gales at the beginning of the year caused havoc particularly along the South Cornwall, South Devon and Dorset coasts. There was far too much to report at length but an item on one small piece near Dartmouth may give an idea of the devastation. 'At Froward Point, near Kingswear, the footpath was blocked after the wind cut a swathe through Monterey Pines growing on the coast. The 90-year-old trees were a familiar and well-loved landmark, and about three-quarters of them were lost. It took the National Trust warden, Mike Ingram, and his team three months to clear away fallen trees so that the coast path could be re-opened'.

Map – Log Books

Brian Panton, a Monroe enthusiast, brought a map of them to a Committee meeting suggesting the Association might like to develop a similar idea for those trying to complete our path. This precise idea did not get off the ground but the idea mutated into the Log Books we now have available. Brian was a keen marathon runner and left one Committee meeting early to be able to travel to London for its Marathon next day. Perhaps though the most surprising fitness story belongs to another of our members, Don Allen. He was also a marathon runner and 100-mile event challenge walker, he arrived one day at an AGM in Newton Abbot in his walking boots. He was jokingly asked if he had walked there, he had in fact done so – he lived in Plymouth!

Walland Carey

We asked in 1989 if the coast path could be routed on the coast between Buck's Mills and Clovelly rather than through the middle of the then Bideford Bay Holiday Camp. The manager at the camp was favourable to the idea and Devon County Council said it would investigate the proposal. It seems such an eminently sensible idea all round that once again one can only despair of the original planners of the path. However these things take time and even though everyone agreed, it was not until 1992 that the route was approved. 'It then took Devon County Council one year to process the line of this new path.' By the spring of 1994 work had not started but the path did open later that year. 'No one else being available your ex-chairman and his wife were dusted off and sent to the official opening. Coffee served in proper cups and saucers on the coast path and a splendid lunch afterwards – they can ask us again! This is a new piece of footpath in North Devon just west of Buck's Mills and east of Clovelly. It is only three-quarters of a mile long it is true, but it is a great improvement on the previous route which ran right through the middle of a holiday camp. Now it goes to seaward, mostly through an old deciduous wood. Thanks for this new piece of path goes several ways: to Hartland Heritage Coast who have been working on the idea for over three years; to Haven Leisure (the camp owners); to the Woodland Trust; and last but not least to Torridge Training Services who supplied so much of the person power to effect the necessary work.

Buckator

The Secretary reported: that on a walk on the north Cornish coast – 'at a rest point at Buckator he watched other walkers pass by and noticed all of them follow the natural line along the cliff and not the official inland path. He has raised this with Cornwall County Council and can report that they are negotiating with landowners to divert the coast path onto the route being walked.' Being fair in this particular place there was a marshy area that gave trouble but the inland diversion was long and seemingly an unlikely way to go. As we had said so often a sensible cliff top route on the coast needed far less signing and waymarking than a contorted illogical route devised by the 'official' mind.

Battern Cliff

Our Association made another attempt to improve this long-standing outstanding flaw in the coast path just west of Portwrinkle on the south Cornish coast. It had been one of those problems that 'will soon disappear' listed by the Countryside Commission at the Cornish opening 17 years ago! The Commission even had the gall, or lack of reality to show on its maps that the path was on the cliffs when in fact you had to walk along the B3247 road. The Commission informed us it was negotiating with the St Germans Parish Council and they assured us that when the problem was resolved they would inform us. In this case there was a long running dispute between the landowner and the local parish council. Our Association failed to see why a local dispute should hold up completion of what was meant to be a national asset, but it did for very many years.

In 1997 the Secretary pointed out that we had been promised this path soon 24 years ago: 'If 24 years is soon then most of us will not be around to walk these alignment improvements. Can anyone wonder with those of us who consider that the coastal experience of walkers is paramount, should be exasperated with coast path managers and the Countryside Commission who promise everything yet rarely produce. All too often we have found that when sensible easy to install path improvements are pointed out, they will agree with our opinions; then – nothing is done.'

In 2000 our Secretary was still complaining there was no path and what added to his annoyance was the fact that the Countryside Agency were not even bothering to answer his letters. He wrote thus; 'can anyone suggest why letters on such important topics should not be dealt with promptly? Maybe we do not carry as much recognition as we thought we had achieved over the past five years or so. Your Secretary and Secretaries before him well remember the innumerable instances this Association was brushed off as a minor nuisance in our early days. It also begs the question –"has the Countryside Agency done anything at all?" We do not know, because no one has bothered to tell us.'

The fine cliff top path finally opened in May 2002. A problem that the Countryside Commission had said would soon disappear had taken no less than 29 years to solve. Is it to be wondered that our Association sometimes feels frustrated? What if every Act of Parliament took so long to implement? 'Councillors county and parish, path managers, tourism people etc. All these gathered to celebrate their success in creating a major essential realignment of the South West Coast Path'. Perhaps though the final comment on this long running saga should be Liz Woollard's 'It goes to show that wonderful things do happen!'

Plymouth Waterfront

In 1990 we had the first news of this forthcoming strategy which would greatly improve the urban walk through Plymouth. It was hoped to reintroduce the ferry from Sutton Harbour to Turnchapel and Mount Batten. The RAF was going to leave Mount Batten and part of 'the area will be set aside for public

Looking across at the Citadel in Plymouth from Mount Batten. The Citadel in Plymouth was built on the orders of Charles II after the Restoration, ostensibly against foreign invasion. However, Plymouth had been a Roundhead stronghold right throughout the Civil War, so some suspected it might at least, in part, have been put there to see there was no further trouble from the local inhabitants!

recreational use which can only mean more coast path'. In 1995 our Secretary was shown a map of the area which had a dotted line for a coastal path all the way round the coastline. There was also news of the MOD leaving King William IV Victualling Yard and the plan eventually to have a coast path there. In 1997 came news that a route had been identified seaward of the road below Staddon Heights, from Jennycliff to join the path to Bovisand. This latter path was to take longer than expected to construct and was not ready by the official opening. It does indeed provide more exercise, but it is so much better than the old road route. The official opening of Mount Batten with a shower of blue and yellow balloons came in March 1998. Our Secretary had the happy thought of inviting all locally living members to attend what was a very happy and significant day out. The Association had a marquee with items for sale and leaflets to distribute, This opening surely proved that sometimes even the seemingly most obdurate of 'unpathed' sections could sometimes become a reality.

As part of the Waterfront strategy Plymouth produced an attractive and informative colour brochure. Amongst other subjects covered was Sir Arthur Conan Doyle's residence in Durnford Street, an order given by Sir John Hawkins, a four foot spanner of Brunel, the shipping of bullion from Millbay Dock, a list of the film-stars and other famous folk who had landed at Plymouth, John Smeaton, him of the lighthouse, and Sir Francis Drake. All in all it proved a real attempt had been made to add interest to this urban walk.

Strete Gate to Warren Cove

This was another of those very long running sagas where we sought to get improvement. Walkers had to walk along stretches of the busy A379 without even the protection of a pavement. Furthermore much of the route was well inland and to say the least of it not scenic. At this stage we had been hopeful of a resolution because the Devon County Council's own Heritage Coast Officer and the Countryside Commission had spent a great deal of time working out an improved route. However Devon County's Environment and Countryside Committee resolved that it was not disposed to make a Public Path Creation Order 'because it considers that certain lengths of such realignment of the existing path would be unduly intrusive upon private property. So there you have it, a handful of private householders take precedence over the thousands who walk the South West Way'. Perhaps what was significant was that the chairperson of the relevant committee lived in that area!

This cartoon from a newsletter highlighted the danger to walkers of having to use the most unsatisfactory inland route from Strete Gate to Warren Point.

It was not until 5 years latter in 1995 that the political log-jam which had held up improvement for so long was broken when a vote, with only one dissension, was taken to consider a more coastal route subject to support from the Countryside Commission. Then much to our chagrin the Countryside Commission refused to fund any improvement. We had constantly aired our views that they would be better to concentrate resources first on finishing existing Long Distance Footpaths before developing new schemes. No one had listened and now there was the opportunity to rectify this long-standing – defect, nothing could be done. As our Secretary put it the Countryside Commission had 'torpedoed Devon County Council's plans to improve the notorious section of the South West Coast Path. The South West Way Association has been striving for a proper coast path in this section for over 20 years. Over the last 18 months Devon County Council has at last accepted its responsibilities and resolved to make the necessary improvements. Now the Countryside Commission has gone weak at the knees in the face of opposition from a few landowners and says it does not have the money. ... Most of the land over which the new route was planned is unused scrubland, field edges and woodlands identical to 90% of the other 600 miles. ... If this is to be an example of the Countryside Commission's approach then the management structure proposed for the future will be doomed to failure.'

The Ramblers' Association Open Britain Day Walk in Devon featured this section, Strete Gate to Warren Point. There was a very good turnout indeed to demonstrate support for a truly coastal path. It was noticeable however how few of the walkers wanted to walk the inland route again on the return, opting instead to queue for buses.

In 1997 the Countryside Commission was still refusing to fund improvements. Its letter stated 'whilst the Commission wants to achieve a satisfactory route in this area, it is not prepared to do so in the face of landowner opposition and in the lights of the costs the Commission would have to carry'. This can hardly be the sort of caveat that Parliament intended when it passed the original Act. Why else would they have given compulsory powers to acquire land for Long Distance Paths? Our Chairman was invited to put the walker's case versus the landowners on BBC Radio 4 *You and Yours* programme.

There was considerable discussion whether we should take the refusal of the Countryside Commission to the Parliamentary Ombudsman. However, having taken advice we decided against that line of approach. It was determined instead to make a joint approach with the Ramblers' Association to the Secretary of State for the Environment, Transport and the Regions, John Prescott, asking him to make a Creation Order. Our Secretary's words:- 'so, patient members, the next round has commenced'. He added an appeal for members to write to their MPs in support.

Unfortunately the Secretary of State refused to make an order. The reply said he was grateful for bringing this matter to his attention and hoped an eventual solution would be found. However a review was set in train asking the South West Coast Path Team to consider options for this stretch of path, obtain clear estimates of the cost of these and agree priority sections of the route where action was required. As part of the review questionnaires were sent to every local household. A series of meetings was held with householders/landowners. A user survey was conducted and conservation bodies consulted. There was an independent road safety audit.

In 2001 the Review Report was published, no less than 85 pages of it. It admitted the lack of coastal enjoyment and perceived danger of walking on road, particularly along stretches of the A379, have resulted in persistent criticism of this section by users of the South West Coast Path. Key conclusions included: current usage of the Strete Gate to Warren Point section is 25% of the level of adjacent sections of the South West Coast Path to the east and west. An alternative route is needed to address safety issues on stretches of main road. The report also admitted this stretch was one of seven pieces identified as a very high priority for realignment by a recent Path Management Survey. More than 50% of this section is on roads which is nearly four times greater than the path average. Only a quarter of the path has any continuous sea view. 87% of visitors and over 62% of residents support the principle of a safer and more enjoyable route. Economic benefit to the area would increase fourfold with a proper coast path. A re-route closer to the sea would not have detrimental effect on archaeology or wildlife. Affected property owners would oppose but they and other locals would like to see the matter settled.

The researchers came to the conclusion that 'a re-route is needed to satisfy road safety, user demand, National Trail quality standards, and to provide a better coastal experience and increase local economic benefit'. Even then despite public opinion being for improvement, both local parish councils voted against! However to give them credit Devon County Council 'commendably accepted the review and recommended it to the Countryside Agency'.

At last in 2001 the Board of the Countryside Agency accepted the report of the South West Coast Path Team to re-route the path; the Agency's officers were authorised to work with Devon County Council to define the best precise line. Our Association played a part in gaining publicity for improvements by providing volunteer walkers to appear on a programme made by Carlton TV. The idea was to show how narrow and dangerous was the main road section of the then present route. This clearly came out in the programme.

1991

Loss last financial Year

The Treasurer reported that for the first time ever the Association had made a loss in its last financial year. The loss was incurred through the increased costs with Devon Books producing the Guide. The Guide this year has been produced by another printer and distributor at much more favourable terms, which is all very fortunate as Devon Books went into liquidation earlier this year.

Heritage Coasts – Policies and Priorities

The Heritage Coast idea had been around for some years now and had been spreading. There now came out a list of six targets which it was hoped would be obtained by 2000. These targets were:

> To create a continuous coastal path along the length of every heritage coast and to ensure that all rights of way in heritage coast areas are properly managed.
> To protect and manage all significant landscape features and important areas for nature conservation.
> To create a coastal strip of semi-natural vegetation along all heritage coasts.
> To remove eyesores.
> To clear litter on a regular basis.
> To designate all heavily used beaches as bathing beaches, which should meet EC standards of water quality.

Although we noticed with considerable interest possibly the first ever official mention of a 'continuous' path, our Secretary's comment was:- 'our Association supports wholeheartedly this policy statement and has asked the Countryside Commission if our large organisation can be of any assistance. I know that every one of the six aims for the year 2000 will be welcomed by all coast users and I feel should the Countryside Commission and the other authorities involved achieve the first target we should have a true coast path along Great Britain's longest long distance trail.'

Visual improvement and otherwise

In this year the caravan site at Beesands was cleared. Whilst it was undoubtedly ugly, particularly in its latter years, it did bring business and work into an isolated community. Commuters and second homeowners have now as elsewhere become the majority. Caravan sites have in other places such as Orcombe Point at Exmouth also gone and this has led to visual improvement. The National Trust has been particularly good at removing old eyesores. On the other hand vast new developments and giant wind turbines have certainly not added to the beauty of views from the coast path. Yet again sometimes as at Brixham new development, a marina and new housing, has been married with the introduction of a harbour-side walk which has been added to the coast path. This is a great improvement of the former walk along the road. What is needed on the coast is a law similar to the London Thames rule that any riverside development must incorporate a riverside path. If we had this on the coast we would in time regain nearly all the coastal path that has been lost to modern building.

Brixham was historically and remains a fishing port. It is remembered as the landing place of William of Orange in his successful bid to replace James II in 1688. The Rev Henry Lyte who wrote Abide with Me *was an incumbent here.*

Culbone

There had been long running problems in this area, admittedly one of unstable cliffs. However as so often with Exmoor National Park they always seemed to be trying to get the path as far away from the coast as possible. For instance because of the possibility of a slip in the area they wanted to close the easy to walk attractive lower path through the woodlands that was about one and a quarter miles long. In its place they wished to substitute a six-mile route which meant walking up the narrow toll road with its enormous climb. Andrew Bristow was our hard-working committee member in that area. We were not the only ones to object: one objector you might expect was the Ramblers' Association and one you might not was the priest in charge of Culbone Church. Exmoor National Park closed our preferred route on a 'temporary basis' for six years but then reopened it in 1995. Closure notices were again in place by 1997 although the path was still walkable. It was open again by 2000.

Kingswear Information Office

Kingswear had an information office opposite the landing point of the Lower Ferry that is used by a large number of walkers. Sensibly as the office was in sight of the coast path they featured it in their window with a signpost replica. Unfortunately they showed it pointing the wrong way! One might have thought an information office would know which way the path went! We took the matter up to get it altered.

Animals to improve the Coastal Corridor

We were advised by the National Trust that:- 'once again about twelve Dartmoor ponies will be taking their winter holidays on the coast at Froward Point near Kingswear. The ponies are invaluable for keeping down scrub and bracken, thus allowing a wide variety of grasses and wild flowers to flourish.' This type of grazing was tried out in a number of other places sometimes with ponies at other times with Soay (St Kilda) sheep. It can easily be forgotten that in times past the coastline was much more intensively used than it is now. Later a small herd of British native goats was introduced at Berry Head by the Torbay Countryside Trust. As June Haywood put it:- 'they are a source of interest rather than a hazard to walkers, although the fencing (erected to protect the public and the goats from each other whilst they become acclimatised) is rather an eyesore until it weathers a bit'.

Four-legged lawnmowers! This is a Dartmoor pony on the west coast of the Lizard. Animals are being used to keep down scrub and to try and restore cliff top land to the state it used to be, when there was more grazing on the coast. It is hoped that this will bring back species of flowers, insects and birds. The chough, with its marvellous tumbling flight has come back to Cornwall after many years' absence.

Dorset

There had been problems at Osmington Mills caused by a landslip. Dorset County Council had gone for a very long and unnecessary diversion. But as Brian Panton reported:- 'however here it is not necessary to follow the official diversion as a rough route is becoming established through the area of landslip. This alternative route has been included in the Association's Annual Guide this year. The Association is continuing to press the authorities for a resolution.' There was also a threat of a Wind Farm with 26 turbines south of Martinstown on the inland route behind Weymouth. 'While the Association supports the idea of the use of renewable energy sources, the siting of this project in such a sensitive and exposed area in an Area of Outstanding National Beauty is not acceptable. Objections have been lodged against the application.'

Officer change

At the end of the year Philippa Dalzell resigned as assistant membership secretary and Liz Wallis, Eric's wife, was appointed in her place.

1992

In the early part of the year there was a meeting with professional consultants employed by the Countryside Commission to look at Long Distance Trails. One asked us what we would most like to see as improvement/alterations to the South West Way. Our immediate reply was a completed coast path. The Committee Meeting that later discussed the matter listed four items:-

A completed coast path
More and better waymarking through towns
Standardisation of waymarking
A quicker reaction by the authorities to difficulties about over-long diversions.

They also mentioned specifically Strete Gate to Warren Cove and Seaton/Bindon Cliff in east Devon.

Finance

Last year 1991 had been a good year financially making up for the poor one in 1990. We had quite a large sum invested to service life members and it was thought wise to keep a 'nest egg' in case we should need to fight a large public enquiry. Ron Vinnicombe pointed out it would cost something like £200 a day to employ a QC.

Committee Changes

Joan Westaway, a Committee member since our inception and ex-chairman, resigned from the Committee. Ron Vinnicombe who had been with us a number of years and led for us at a number of enquiries also stood down. Ann Richards from Dorset and Ron Bagshaw from Devon joined the Committee.

Secretary's Report

He had been asked about the increase of walkers upon the coast path; was it in part due to it being the longest Long Distance Trail? He thought there were other reasons too:- 'I believe the South West Way draws walkers to it for its spectacular beauty, its rugged and at times isolated grandeur, the quiet coves, friendly locals and our good welcoming west country B & Bs'. He also commented on the changing agricultural situation and its possible relevance. 'In recent years there has been a radical reappraisal by Government into our countryside. Evidence of this is the document "Action for the Countryside" and their policy on set aside. It is reported that 15% of Great Britain's farmland is surplus to requirement. There are a number of sections along the South West Way where we have no true coast path. If set aside was implemented in those areas then both the coast path user and the local farmer would benefit. In the past we have been told that agriculture has priority over coast path. We ask; does this apply now?'

Richard Butler, the Countryside Manager for Devon County Council, gave the talk after the AGM.

Cumbria Coast Path

We were approached by authorities in Cumbria who were keen to establish a coast path there. They contacted us as a user group, asking for advice, and we had been pleased to provide it.

This is the breach through the shingle bank at Porlock Bay. Our Association had no quarrel with the National Rivers Authority wish to let nature take its course. We did however think a much more robust attitude should have been taken to making a new truly coastal path.

Porlock Bay

We were advised that the National Rivers Authority was contemplating flooding the coastline adjacent to Porlock Bay. The area had been flooded some 18 months previously and it was thought that nature should be allowed to take its course to the advantage of wildlife. In 1996 a combination of high tides and high winds led to further problems. The worst breach was a wide deep channel through the shingle ridge and coast path. On high tides the sea rushed through into the marsh behind. If we had known how much of a problem it was going to be to establish anything like a reasonable new coast path we would have been more perturbed then than we were. Exmoor's first answer was a path inland even of the main road and disagreeable too in that it followed a drain. In the spring of 2003 our Secretary reported thus:- 'a new path has been officially opened that avoids a diversion through Porlock. We did have the impression that Exmoor National Park was quite happy for the diverted route along roads and through the town to become the official route. However all's well that ends well. Thank you Exmoor National Park. Watch out for new direction signs.' Unfortunately our Secretary's optimism was not entirely justified; at the current time there are still problems in the area.

Worthygate Wood

The original path from Gauter's Pool to Buck's Mills had a loop inland to make use of an existing right of way rather than keeping closer to the coast. We suggested that 'the path need not leave the woodlands to track inland then follow that high hedged lane down into Buck's Mills'. The National Trust acquired the land and soon constructed a new more direct route through the woods for which we had asked ten years previously.

Clovelly

It was announced that a new path was to be cut from the Hobby Drive just west of its termination directly down into the village. This was not our idea but certainly one of which we greatly approved because we hoped more walkers would be encouraged to descend to see this beautiful village; a village as someone once said 'like a waterfall'.

Port Quin

We suggested to the National Trust that simply by making a new entry in its property wall just west of Port Quin a length of path could be taken off the road leading out behind Doyden Castle. They moved so quickly on this one that we lost the opportunity to suggest the optimum place for the gap. We did get a better route but it could have been even better.

Doyden Castle, near Port Quin has extensive cellars and was once reputedly the scene of wild parties. Now it is rented accommodation. There were antimony mines nearby, this metallic element has been used to produce the yellow colour in stained glass as well as in a number of alloys.

East Devon Way

Dennis Martin our committee member for east Devon had been invited to the opening of the East Devon Way, a walk of about 40 miles from Exmouth to Uplyme close to Lyme Regis in Dorset. It was suggested in their guide that there was the opportunity of making a round trip by returning by the coast path.

Everest Three Times

In 1992 the Chairman and his wife Mary walked the whole of the path as a retirement present to each other. 'We had started walking stretches together when we were first married. Later with a growing family, some of it was done as push-chair walks, and then, more adventurously, as Youth Hostel expeditions. The Association's inception meant walking with a more serious purpose in mind and, of course, the necessity of walking the path systematically. This year's walk therefore was bound to be one of reassessment and nostalgia.

The Good Things – Improvements

The path, on the whole, is better maintained than it has ever been. ... We particularly appreciated the waymarking posts in North Cornwall which told you where you were on the shank. ... The new National Trail Guides by Aurum Press, though not flawless are the best series of guide books we have yet handled. ... Improvements in routing, taking one nearer the sea ... the re-established regular ferry from St Mawes to Place was a boon.

The Bad Things – Grumbles

There are still the three major gaps ... East Coast of the Lizard ... Portwrinkle ... Strete Gate to Little Dartmouth. ... There are also literally dozens of small gaps where one has to walk along a road, and yet there are fields to seaward. ... There are still some areas where waymarking and maintenance are disgraceful.

The Logistics and Method

No South West Way fan now needs to be told that the path is over 600 miles long, 613 in fact at our last count. However, some approximation of the total climbing has always intrigued us, so we spent a little evening time trying to count contours. ... We have come up with a minimum figure of some 91 000 feet; hence the title "Everest Three Times" (we are sure we have not got the full total).

We started on the 2nd of May and finished in mid-June. We chose that time because of the flowers, but we were also extremely lucky with the weather. We only had one nearly whole wet day, two half wet days and a few showers.

Bluebells are so prolific in woodlands and at many places along the coast. Some times there are considerable drifts of whitebells. Bluebell bulbs were once used to make glue for bookbinding and for starch.

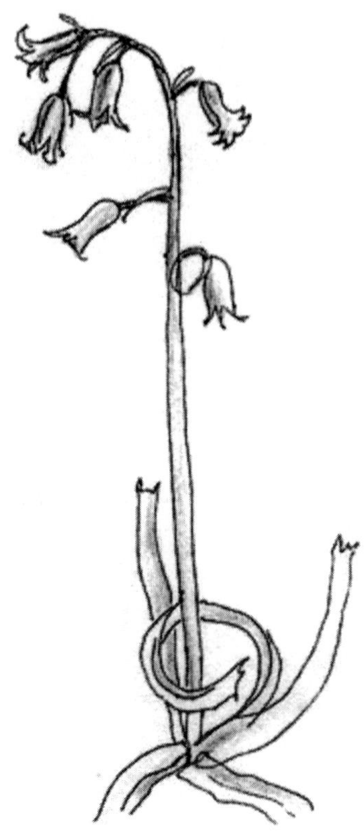

The Highlights and Memories

We especially remember the other walkers we met and the laughs shared. We met more foreigners than ever before, for example several from Holland and Germany, a biggish party from America as well as individuals.

We walked through the developing seasons ... we saw some of the earliest bluebells and later they were all over. When I saw our first cowslip I called Mary back to see it, I need not have bothered as in a few days we passed hundreds. The most ubiquitous flower was the sea-pink ... and the yellow kidney vetch ... scarlet poppies ... delighted the eye, and once we saw a completely white one, a rarity or freak.

Conclusion – the End

Having suggested to so many others that they should go and walk it, it was only fair that we too should set out on this longest of all our National Trails. Thus we went, we mostly enjoyed it, and we shall have memories to share as long as we live.'

Mary added a postscript. 'It was, all-in-all a good and memorable adventure and we were glad that we did it. ... There were only four days out of the 45 when I sincerely wished that I was somewhere else, indeed ANYWHERE else, but that's not a bad percentage, and we are still married!

One last thought, although we are lucky to enjoy both good health and the means to have made this long trek, it is a wonderful feeling to unlock your front door and know that you are home again, and can go to sleep in your own bed'.

1993

This was the Association's twentieth birthday and at the AGM there was a special cake on which even the boots and rucksack decorations were edible!

The Chairman had this to say of the twenty years' efforts:- 'Today, a lot of the splendid path you walk has had the direct input of your Association, and we hope you enjoy it as much as we do and feel proud that you have helped in its completion. On other stretches we have not yet won the argument but at least folks – twenty years on, we are still fighting.' He also thanked the officers and Committee for their work for our organisation saying 'it is your Secretary Eric who carries the biggest load'. Frederick White stood down from his position as Vice-Chairman and Brian Panton was elected in his place. Frederick White however continued as a Committee member. Ann Richards gave her first report on Dorset, she had a way with words and her first description of the Lyme Regis Golf Course diversion was:- 'lung-choking, traffic-dodging, foot-blistering, road-walking'. She also mentioned that:- 'the annual Dorset Beach clean yielded 900 sacks of litter – as well as 22 car tyres'.

Meeting Countryside Commission

In view of the better relations we had enjoyed with the Countryside Commission it was thought that the Chairman and Secretary should request a meeting in Bristol with the head of their office there. This was arranged and was to be the beginning of a useful dialogue although the first meeting proved to be disappointing.

Reverse Guide

We had considered the idea before of a Reverse Guide written from Poole to Minehead and then turned it down. However in view of a continuing number of requests we changed our minds and decided to produce one, hoping to have it available in 1994. It was however decided that it would only be the trail description that would be written in reverse and that it would not be produced annually. All other information would stay in the main guide as now. Preparation of this new guide meant that volunteers had to walk the path 'backwards' and it did prove 'How very poor the waymarking is "the other way"'. The Reverse Guide was updated in 1998, 2002 and 2004.

Ferries

The vastly increased insurance required by ferry operators nearly brought a halt to the ferry across the Yealm. Happily Devon County Council stepped into the breach. Sadly in this litigious age it has become quite impossible to run a small ferry as a commercial operation unless it is subsidised. The Association has for some years been working out and writing up walking routes around estuaries, especially those that only have a seasonal ferry service. In fact it has advocated that these routes around should become part of the coast path. The authorities have resisted this presumably on the grounds of cost although they set a precedent themselves on the river Torridge by taking the path down to Bideford.

Welcombe Mouth

There were fears over a possible caravan and camping site development at Welcombe Mouth, with its delightfully named stream Strawberry

The delightfully named Strawberry Water in flash flood at Welcombe Mouth. In Edwardian days when church was obligatory for local children at Welcombe they occasionally had a reprieve. The local parson was responsible for Lundy. Some times when they went to church, the Church Warden would get up and announce 'Parson's gone to Lundy, won't be back to Monday'. The children could hardly cheer, but immediately, happily, trooped out again.

Water. It was, however, hoped that as this area was now part of a Heritage Coast the matter would be resolved.

Bridge at the mouth of the River Otter

We had originally asked if a pedestrian bridge could be built here. We had later abandoned the idea because it was felt it might interfere with bird life. Ron Bagshaw thought there would in fact be fewer disturbances for the birds simply crossing at the mouth of the river rather than walking along both sides of the estuary. It was therefore decided to try and reopen the matter.

1994

South West Coast Path Project

This survey was set up by the Countryside Commission to work out a long term plan for the coast path. It was to consider how the path was used, the condition it was in, and the economic benefits that it brought. It involved the Countryside Commission, the local authorities, the National Trust and our Association. It had at last been appreciated that the path would benefit from integrated management and co-ordinated publicity. Firstly however there was a need to gather information about the present state of the path. It was in part funded by European money and was expected to take two years.

There would be two main aspects to the survey. Teams of interviewers, at various times and different locations would question walkers and the results would be collated on computer. We appealed for volunteers to act as interviewers. Others would actually walk the path recording the condition of its surface, the waymarking, stiles, gates etc. It was hoped that the survey would be complete by the spring of 1996. There were to be five topic groups:- 1) Public Transport, 2) Tourism, 3) Landscape/ Wildlife/ Heritage, 4) Voluntary/ Community Involvement, and 5) Alignment/ Legalities. The Association's Chairman and Secretary would have representation on 4) and 5). Later other members represented us on the other three topic groups.

'We acknowledge our special position in our involvement as the only member representing the user of the coast path. We hope to be able to make positive and practical contributions.' Furthermore as our Secretary said: 'There may be individual officers who know their section of the coast path better, but there is nobody that knows all of the coast path better than the South West Way Association'.

In Dorset during the summer of 1994 the path usage survey had consisted of 250 hours of interviewing and over 1000 people registered their walks in self-registration boxes. Interviewers near Berry Head in Devon found that the numbers willing to complete forms increased dramatically by providing folding chairs at the census point! In one day they had through a two week old baby, admittedly not actually walking, and a spry 91 year-old who was proceeding briskly and climbed a stile without trouble. One volunteer's comment was as follows:- 'Although it is true we had volunteered we still viewed the first session with a little trepidation. We wondered what peoples' reaction would be to being stopped whilst out on a walk. We had not always welcomed market research types when shopping. Would we get the brush off? In fact folk could not have been nicer, nearly all of them were happy to stop and patiently answer the questions.' A Dorset interviewer wrote:- 'In return for a completed interview, we shared pizza, coffee and lent him (a walker) our treasured 1972 War Department army can opener to take on his walk to Land's End – he returned it in a Christmas card five months later. Bless him.'

The first results from the survey were interesting and held some surprises. The total number of people using the path during the time of the survey was estimated to be over 1 million, 1 074 094 to be exact. Walkers were divided into two categories – those just out for a day or less, SDW, and those walking for more than a day, LDW. The vast majority were SDW 93%. Of the LDW 5% were walking the whole path. 44% of holidaymakers said the existence of the trail was a factor in visiting the area.

Category	SDW	LDW
Overseas visitors	6%	7%
Full-time occupations	57%	61%
Retired	18%	14%
Walking alone	19%	34%
Accompanied by children	20%	5%
Males	57%	64%
Scenery – main attraction	63%	93%

Land's End has been the ambition of so many, let us tell you about just one. In 1960 Billy Butlin held his walking race from John o' Groats to Land's End. The oldest person to finish was a widow, Maud Nicholas 62 from Camelford. She averaged 30 miles a day carrying her 'bag of eats'. She improved as she went along, so they had to ask her to slow up on the last stage or she would have reached Land's End before her welcoming coach party of local Penzance OAPs!

As an adjunct to the main survey a questionnaire was circulated to all our members. Some 333 replied giving a return rate of 20% that was pleasing. Of these 9% had not walked any of the path in the last year. 35% had spent 6 – 10 days and 34% more than 10 days. The greatest attraction was scenery 70% though some said 'challenge' and others 'peace and quiet' or 'nature, birds, wildlife'. Asked what spoilt the walk the biggest grumble was having to walk on roads. Others disliked the weather, and inland diversions. For finding the way 84% used waymarks, 78% OS maps, 66% our Guide, 44% our Path Descriptions, and 31% the National Trail Guides. 63% walked with family and friends, 27 alone and 7% with walking clubs.

A lot of members had walked on other Long Distance Paths; Pennine Way 43%, Pembrokeshire Coast Path 40%, Offa's Dyke 39% South Downs Way 35% and The Ridgeway 32%. No less than 23% had walked long distance trails in other countries abroad. There was, however, an exclusive number who had walked no other long distance path but ours – 5%. Nearly three-quarters thought waymarking was adequate but over a quarter thought it was insufficient. Satisfaction rates certainly varied: those satisfied with Leaflets/Guides was 85%, with Maintenance 75%, Accommodation 67%, Car Parking 46% but Public Transport only 19%. Asked about Improvements required, the biggest request was moving the path nearer to the coast in some areas. The Length of Walk divided into 14% who had walked over 100 miles, 25% 51 – 100 miles, and 28% 1 – 10 miles. The biggest expenditure on the trail was on accommodation, food and drink from cafés and pubs came next, closely followed by purchases from shops.

By 1995 we began to discuss what the Association's role would be if as the result of the coast path project a different management structure emerges. The Chairman thought that the Association should be involved. 'There are more advantages to be gained by being in at the centre of activity than not. Should the occasion arise the Association would reserve the right to disagree with the management authority as and when we feel it correct to do so.' He went on to say that the Steering Group really does look to the Association to reflect the users' interests. The Chairman also made these points about the Association's work:- 'your work has been acknowledged by the various organisations and authorities involved in the Project, and has done much to raise the recognition and status of the Association as the principal organisation representing users of the South West Way. It is now accepted that the South West Way Association's overall knowledge of matters affecting the entire route cannot be surpassed.'

Consultation Draft

This was received only just in time for it to have a write-up in the spring 1996 newsletter. 'Briefly some of the more important proposals of the Strategy in so far as the South West Way is concerned are as follows:-

The establishment of a South West Coast Path Committee (representing a wide make-up of interests) to provide leadership and promote the entire coast path as a single identity.

The reconstruction of the Project Steering Group as the South West Coast Path Management Group to advise the Committee and co-ordinate trail management and marketing.

The formation of a small team of four full-time staff to support and service the Committee and Management Group.

The production of a five year Business Plan for the coast path which is reviewed annually and which incorporates the Local Management Plan produced by the 58 Local Strategy Areas.

The development of a voluntary warden scheme for the coast path.
A substantial improvement is needed to have the path on its correct designated alignment, on rights of way and off roads.

The adoption of standards for path maintenance, signing and waymarking.
Moves to designate and sign the route through urban areas.

Improvements to ferries and estuaries and alternative estuary routes.

The acknowledgement made of the role already made by the South West Way Association as a provider of information and other services, and the suggestion to provide support to the Association to assist in a management and marketing role.

It would be easy to add that several of these points were just the ones we had been making for years without any need to

Place Manor in Cornwall, a ferry runs here from St Mawes. In front of Place Manor was the site of a one time tidal mill. It seems a good idea to harness the tide, but the tide was master, determining the periods when it was possible to mill and this moved daily. It was no sinecure being a tidal miller.

carry out a survey. However if the recommendations were carried out we could hope for a better future for the path. 'But ... the worry is – will there be sufficient financial resources available to achieve the objectives?'

Condition Survey

'The Condition Survey has produced a number of interesting statistics which hitherto have probably never been published for the entire path.'

Natural surfaces 60%, Man-made surfaces, tarmac, concrete and improved, 40%.

Stiles 941, gates 382, bridges 423, steps 22 018.

The Association argued with total distance, the Survey posited it was 561 miles compared to our then 613. They had omitted the urban areas despite the fact they had acknowledged they needed to be signed and were of course usually walked.

Despite this first interesting information the full Condition Survey was still not published three years later. It was then admitted that the Survey had not been satisfactory. There had been a lack of standardisation. Only the route shown in the National Trail Guides had been surveyed, not the actually aligned route. It was therefore decided that it would have to be done again more satisfactorily. In 1999 it was announced that global positioning equipment would be used to carry out a through survey of the path. The equipment had already been used in a trial in Cornwall.

The Final Strategy when it came out was called 'More than just a Path' and it was endorsed by the Association's Committee at the end of 1996. The Steering Group then moved on and became the South West Coast Path Management Group. 'Its primary role will be to oversee and implement the management strategy. A South West Coast Path Team was created to monitor and manage the finances and prepare budgets for the maintenance and management of the coast path. It will also advise and prepare reports for the South West Coast Path Forum. ... A South West Coast Path Forum will be set up to advise on the policy for the coast path and oversee the implementation of the strategy. It would not be involved with day-to-day management or financial matters. It will maintain a strong commitment to the overall strategic decision making and will also have a key role to liaise with outside interests.' The Association was to be represented on both the Management Group and the Forum.

Perhaps the new outlook is largely encapsulated in this paragraph.

More than Just a Path

As the title says, the South West Coast Path is more than just a path. Visitors come to enjoy the natural, historic and cultural aspects of the surrounding landscape (the "corridor" of the path). These things provide all the wonderful sights, sounds and experiences to which the path gives unrivalled access. Enjoyment of the coast path is as much about these things as it is about the path surface, stiles and signs. Users need these services offered by local communities: accommodation, loos, refreshments, public transport, and so on. As walkers and supporters of the coast path you will be fully aware of these things. But the way that the path is currently funded and managed does not always reflect this wider picture.

A new logo was designed which it was hoped would increase awareness.

This was the new coast path logo designed to increase awareness. Has it?

Fourth Chairman

At the AGM Brian Panton from Dorset was elected to be the fourth Chairman of the Association. Frederick White was re-elected to his former position as Vice-Chairman. The new Chairman said: 'I am very much aware of the responsibilities that you have entrusted in me and hope that I will be able to justify the confidence expressed by my proposers. I can assure you all that I will serve the Association to the best of my ability. Although my style may be different, my principal objectives – the further improvement of the South West Coast Path and the growth and influence of the Association will be the same.' He also said he had to admit – 'that I have not yet completed the entire path – a matter that will be put right by the end of the year'. Eric Wallis was later to say of him, 'his skill at translating and deciphering official documents and papers is, as far as I am concerned, unequalled'.

The retiring Chairman said 'We started this Association for two basic reasons; the authorities were dragging their feet over completing the path, and, walkers were not being allowed any say in its creation. They just did not want to know what the customers' opinion was.

'Someone once said to me "Do you think that what you have done for the South West Way has been worth all the work and hassle?" I replied I have only to walk along the coast from Kingswear to Brixham, where you may remember, Devon County Council and the Countryside Commission opposed a path. To know just that – it has been worth it. There is still much to be done but at least there is a better path now than there would have been if there had been no Association.'

The Secretary in his report said; 'Members will be interested to know we now have members in Australia, Canada, France, Germany, Holland, Luxembourg, South Africa, Sweden, Switzerland and the USA; in fact America has more members than any of the others put together.' Ann Richards in her report on Dorset reminded us:- 'there are always two views; the one behind and the one ahead of you'.

Committee Meetings it was decided would in future start in the mornings and no longer be held in a private house. They were still to be held in Newton Abbot but a few years later they were moved to Exeter, close to the railway station.

Banks & Building Societies

We had for some while been publishing information about banks and building societies around the path. This was important for those making extended trips around the path in the days before cash machines became common. In 1994 two of our members S Lane of Croydon and S Whaley of Chessington separately worked out a complete analysis. It must have taken them a considerable amount of time. We published the results in the spring Newsletter. We did also add the reminder that a Giro account was still probably the easiest way to obtain cash as still every town and most villages then had a post office.

An Accolade for the Secretary

The Chairman had received a letter from Minnesota USA:- 'We recently returned from a two week backpacking trip along the South West Coast Path from Minehead to Padstow. During the months of preparation for this trip we corresponded quite a bit with Eric Wallis. This is a short note to let you know how much we have been impressed with Eric. Unfortunately we have never met him. But we found his correspondence always very informative, fun, full of good information, and prompt. His letters conveyed a real personal interest in us and what we wanted to accomplish, which made us feel valuable and therefore all the more excited to come to England for the walk. You have a valuable man in Eric'.

Chivenor

We had news that the RAF base at Chivenor near Braunton in North Devon would be closed. We wrote saying that if this did come to pass we would like to see the coast path extended around that site. In fact the base has not closed and there is no indication that it may do so in the immediate future.

Penzance Station

South West Water had been carrying out major works in the area of Penzance railway station. We thought this was an opportunity to eliminate a stretch of road walking and having to cross the busy main road by keeping the path to seaward of the railway line. Encouragingly Cornwall County Council seemed interested in the idea. It was to take half a dozen years or so before the good idea was to be implemented as an improvement. When it finally came into effect it was also a cycleway.

Computerisation

We learnt that a grant of 50% was available from the Countryside Commission to assist the Association in a purchase of our first computer. Acknowledgement had of course to be made of the Commission's grant. The computer would certainly earn its keep but the fact it was needed, was proof indeed of how much the Association had grown and the amount of work undertaken. In fact we had only survived this long without one because we had been making use of the Membership Secretary's! We had in fact worn out her printer so we bought her a new one.

Cornish Report

We had a report from one of our Cornish Representatives that surely needs to be remembered. 'he had been walking the remote sections on the North Cornwall coast. From Port Isaac to Trebarwith Strand, and from Boscastle to High Cliff and Crackington Haven. So what do I have to report? These sections are tough and they are beautiful. That was to be my report – what more do you want?'

The Commission Chairman and the House of Lords

The Secretary received a letter from Sir John Johnson, the Chairman of the Countryside Commission. He said he had walked part of the path in South Devon and had purchased one of our guides. He wrote:- 'I was greatly impressed by the amount of detailed information in it. Your

This peaceful stream became a raging torrent in 2004. The small Youth Hostel is the second building beyond the bridge. Boscastle's name originates from Bottreaux castle which is no longer extant.

members put in a great deal of work which is much appreciated by the many people who walk the National Trail. A member of the House of Lords was telling me this week that he and his wife are spending this summer walking the Trail in sections.'

White House, Crow Point, near Braunton, Devon. An example of the work of Sue Jeffreys, she sketched as she walked and later generously donated her work to our Association.

Sue Jeffreys' Walk

Sue Jeffreys started walking the Path in May 1994 and made an illustrated journal as she journeyed. She later generously donated the use of these drawings to our Association.

1995

The AGM

At the meeting the Chairman spoke of the hopes of adding Portland but then had this to say of suggestions of adding on to the ends of the path. 'We have avoided enthusiasm for other additions as they will consume vast amounts of money and if there is money available for additions then those responsible should think about completing our coast path before adding to it. Here we are 12 months on and the line of the coast path has not been improved at Kenidjack, St Loy, south of Mousehole, Chynalls Cliff, Godrevy/ Porthoustock/ Porthallow or Downderry to Portwrinkle all in Cornwall. The same applies to Devon at Strete Gate to Warren Point which still qualifies as being the South West Coast Path and they have still to come up with a coast path east of Seaton from the River Axe to Bindon Cliff. After all, it is supposed to be a coast path yet councils, having the power to create, seem disinterested in the idea.'

The Secretary reported the first member from Hawaii. Ken Franey the North Devon representative echoed the Chairman's unfinished business theme. 'We still have road walking at Watermouth Cove; the alternative path from Saunton Down to the hotel to avoid the double road crossing, has not been resolved. The totally unacceptable road walk at Saunton and finally the strange road walk at South Hole Cross, where last summer I walked along the cliff at this point and found no reason why there was not a path here, are also unchanged. David Venner the Project Co-ordinator for the coast path gave the talk after the meeting.

Future AGMs

It was decided that, to help more people attend, in future AGMs would not always be held in Newton Abbot. It was thought they could circulate round the different counties through which the path passed. The first one away from Newton Abbot was held in Plymouth in 1997. Subsequently meetings have been held in; Truro, Dorchester, Taunton, Fremington (it should have been at Barnstaple but securing accommodation proved difficult), Exeter, Looe and Paignton.

Sweat Shirts and T-shirts

Our Secretary with a little wit wrote then:- 'Due to popular demand we have at last decided to produce and sell our own shirts bearing the South West Way Association logo. An order form is enclosed. Although we do not possess a "cat walk" the shirts were modelled by a couple of your Committee at our last meeting. Although the models were definitely not anywhere like those of the house of Yves St Laurent or Christian Dior, the shirts looked jolly nice.'

Later the range of merchandise we offered was to grow and include such items as polo shirts, tumblers and tankards. A later more ambitious project was a counted cross-stitch embroidery kit of the coast path designed by Liz Wallis with a chart by John Greensmith. The design was also used for a set of attractive coast path notelets. Later still we were to produce an attractive souvenir leaflet of the merchandise we offered, which made a useful contribution to funds as well as promoting the path.

Internet

The Association joined the Internet thanks to the good work of one of our members, Andrew Lack, and the generous support of City University. We were glad to make a presence on this fast-expanding source of information. Our extensive library of photographic slides was a great asset in making a colourful presentation. Andrew Lack's description:- 'The Internet is a computer network, which in simple terms is to computers what the telephone system is to us humans – it allows any computer connected to the network to "talk" to any other computer so connected. Like the telephone system computers on the Internet have unique numbers.'

Over the years our website has generated a number of enquiries, so thanks to Andrew are due. www.swcp.org.uk is the current address.

World Heritage Site Proposal

In May the Secretary attended a special meeting of the Lyme Bay and Dorset Coastal Forum at Exeter. This meeting was to discuss the possibility of applying for World Heritage status for part of the Devon and Dorset coasts and the likely support for pursuing that aim.

The Candidate Coast

The area has great scientific and educational importance and boasts some of the finest coastal scenery in England. The coast's remarkable geology, superbly displayed in cliff outcrops, spans over 300 million years of the earth's history. The coastline includes some of the best examples of landslips, coves and barrier beaches to be found anywhere in Britain or the world.

Beneath the waves, the sea has a varied and complex marine topography including submerged cave systems and off shore reefs. Associated with these coastal and marine environments is an outstanding range of wildlife communities.

Local Government Reorganisation

The Committee was worried about an increase in the number of unitary local authorities. It was felt the least number of authorities involved with the coast path the easier it would be for the Association.

Porlock Weir and Exmoor

We were successful in persuading the Exmoor National Park to move the coast path from behind a hotel there, to the front i.e. the seaward side. There were existing definitive rights of way both behind and in front. So once again one is baffled by the sheer ineptitude of those who set up the path in the first instance. Why route you past the kitchens with no view, when you could just as easily be routed along in sight of the sea?

This little 'Rhenish' tower is not the original that was sadly swept away at the time of the Lynmouth disaster in 1952. Despite its attractive appearance, it served a mundane purpose, as an inlet for General Rawdon's salt-water baths!

We also achieved the promise of improvements on the lower part of Countisbury Hill at Lynmouth and in the Valley of Rocks at Lynton. Here again the official route was along the road when only yards away was a perfectly acceptable footpath.

Culbone Wood

The path through the wood was reopened after seven years' closure. It had originally been closed because of a landslip and fears there might be another. Thanks were due to Bill Gurnett, Head Ranger of Exmoor, that the long and tedious diversion was no longer to be used.

Sandhole Cliff near Welcombe North Devon

This had been a long outstanding gap in the coast path that was all the more apparent because it came in a long and very satisfactory stretch. This gap necessitated a length of road walking. It was found that three landowners were involved and two were happy for the path to be re-routed off the road along the coast. The third is still resisting.

Varley Head near Port Isaac

Success was obtained in securing the removal of a seaward fence to the coast path, a so-called 'corridor of fenceposts'. The Countryside Commission agreed with us and the removal made very little difference to the landowner but a great deal of difference to walkers.

West Cornwall

The Chairman and Secretary over a two day period travelled extensively with two officials, James MacFarlane and Roger Parrot, looking at our suggested improvements. Several of these have now come into being such as at Portreath and Porthcurno. However, the most useful was at Gwithian where quite a long road walk has been eliminated in favour of a new route crossing the Red River to seaward. A new bridge was required here but it was built within twelve months; a very speedy improvement indeed. Our thanks to all concerned though we did have to point out afterwards that though the new bridge had been built, the signposts still indicated the old road route.

Tregantle Cliff

The National Trust opened up a new path on their land here so eliminating another section of road walking. 'So bang goes another section where hikers are likely to bump into motor cars, thus causing considerable damage. Geoffrey Hicks, the National Trust Warden for this section was responsible for the improvement so we take this opportunity of thanking him on your behalf.'

Torquay

The Committee discussed the coast path, which is owned by the local authority but leased to the Imperial Hotel. This lease of the path means a *de facto* exclusion of people other than hotel guests using the path. It was understood that Dominic Acland was investigating the matter.

Another matter that came to the Committee's attention was the closure of part of the coast path around Thatcher Point. This was caused by a minor landslip but the real problem was that the landowner was known to be abroad and not able to be contacted. There seems to be a serious defect in the law here that nothing can be done to secure the couple of yards needed to move back the path in the owner's absence. This dispute is still unresolved at the time of writing, nearly ten years later. What is needed is obviously something like a 'rolling path' agreement.

1996

Newcomers

Liz Woollard and Geoff Davis joined the Committee. Frederick White stepped down from Vice-Chairman and Andrew Bristow was elected in his place. Frederick however continued to serve on the Committee. The Secretary reported on a significant new departure: the cover of the coast path's draft strategy had the legend 'Minehead 613 miles' which was the first time there had been an official recognition of our estimate for the total distance. Until this point officialdom had consistently under-called the true length of the path. Ann Richards mused aloud on the work of Committee members:- 'We look at the stars – we continue to be involved in the huge process of the South West Coast Path Strategy ... we get our suits on, travel afar, and hear lofty talk of 13 million pounds' regional tourism bids. But we also look down – we get our boots on, get the maps out and discuss the path on the site, on the path. And most importantly, we still all walk it – we are a "feet on" organisation. This gives us the local, the immediate and relevant knowledge – the very reason that the South West Way Association input has been so valuable.' Mary Carter told the meeting that she understood from the Membership Secretary that a recent article in the *Guardian* newspaper had generated over 400 enquiries.

Thatcher Rock is an impressive islet in Tor Bay. Torquay is a relatively new town and in part owes it growth to the fleet often being based here during the Napoleonic Wars. Plymouth Sound, the regular naval base was not a safe anchorage, in all states of the wind in days of sail, before the Breakwater was built. Later Torbay was sometimes used for reviews of the Fleet.

Colour slides of the coast path

A keen member for many years, Mr John Kent of Welling, generously bequeathed his collection of thousands of coloured slides of the coast path to

This was the map postcard the Association eventually produced designed by Bryan Cath. It shows the whole coast path and some of the interesting places along it.

our Association. Our Secretary made the journey to collect them. Our Secretary wrote; – 'These, together with my own and some given by others to the Association, now has become quite a massive collection. It probably is the largest in the world. The more we think about it the more we are convinced that we are the ideal organisation to become archive holders of pictures.' The Secretary later announced the collection amounted to some 6000 slides and a special slide storage system had to be obtained.

Postcards

The provision of postcards was discussed at Committee meetings. One idea was a map, another was a composite card with several views on it. The idea was again discussed in 1998; it was then thought that the sales of descriptions might give an indication to the most popular areas of the path and therefore a lead for producing postcards.

Tintagel

We had been asking that the permissive footpaths around the two Penhallic Points, East and West, both west of Tintagel should become the true coast path rather than the official slightly more inland route. This was agreed with all concerned on what was mostly National Trust land.

Hallsands

Unfortunately there had been further erosion here so that the path down to the old village was closed. This had not in fact been part of the coast path so in principal not in our remit. However we did feel sorry about it because the ill-fated ruined village was certainly a draw and visited by many passing walkers.

St Materiana Church at Tintagel is close to the coast path and an entrance gate has a Cornish stile which one feels must have been the inspiration for the modern cattle grid. In Cornish tri-syllable place names the emphasis is usually on the second syllable hence Tintagel.

Sidmouth

On Peak Hill just to the west of Sidmouth there had been a series of landslips. At first this necessitated crossing the road down the hill but later the road itself was endangered and a new one had to be made inland. This time happily the path was again put on the seaward side, the option we always prefer. There were also problems on Salcombe Hill to the east of Sidmouth but these were more intractable.

Poole

Poole Borough Council erected a sign at North Haven Point, not on the coast path but on the opposite side of the ferry from the finish at South Haven Point. It pointed across the mouth of Poole Harbour and reads 'South West Coast Path'. Our Secretary wrote:- 'Well done Poole Borough Council ... they have achieved more than the combined efforts to date of Dorset County Council, Purbeck District Council, Countryside Commission and National Trust, who could collectively, or singularly, have made some contribution to signing or information boards at South Haven Point. Now at least many of the thousands of summer visitors heading for the beaches of Shell Bay and Studland will know of the existence of the South West Coast Path.'

A car ferry leaving Poole Harbour. If your excitement at having reached South Haven Point is not so great as to blot out everything else it can be quite diverting to watch the various shipping. The most mundane but the most obvious being the chain ferry to Sandbanks and home!

Chapter 7

To Our Silver Jubilee and Beyond 1997–2003

1997

Countryside Commission – The Way Forward

In view of the Association's increasing workload the Chairman proposed that we should amongst other things formulate an annual and a five-year business plan. There was possibly the need for additional officers for specific duties e.g. publications, press publicity, events editors etc. When this was about to be discussed in detail there was an invitation from Nick Holliday of the Countryside Commission for the Association's officers to meet him and discuss what role the Association could play in the future. In view of the invitation the discussion was postponed. Delegates were later to say they thought the meeting had been helpful and interesting. They sensed a turnaround of attitude by the Countryside Commission. It was suggested that, with a grant from the Commission, a 'facilitator' should be employed to produce a 'development plan'.

Marketing later Merchandising Officer

A new recruit Mike Farrell volunteered to become a Marketing Officer to promote the various lines of merchandise we already sold. He was formally elected in the following year. He would also seek out and suggest additional ones. One specific proposal was a Log Book detailing the path so walkers could complete them as they finished specific sections.

Overseas Members

The AGM this year was different in two respects. It was held at The Plymouth Athenaeum, the first time it had not been held in Newton Abbot. The other first was that two overseas members attended – they were Sheila and Carl Litsinger from the USA. The Secretary had in a previous report mentioned walkers from overseas he now had known of walkers from these additional countries Austria, Belgium, Israel and Italy. There was also later in the meeting the report of an Australian who wrote 'the South West Way ... worth travelling across the world to walk'. Liz Woollard who had just completed writing a description Mevagissey to Fowey made a wry comment on the advantage of off road paths. 'It was during the writing of this description that I discovered that perhaps the greatest reason for taking the coast path off the main road in Par is to prevent embarrassment to the path description writer walking through the town with mini tape recorder and microphone!' The talk after the meeting was given by Derek James, Plymouth's Coastal Officer on 'Closing a gap in the coast path'.

Explorer Maps

The splendid new 'Explorer' maps were continuing to come out: eventually they will cover the entire coast path that shows up clearly on them. As our Secretary said these were far superior to the old 'Pathfinders' they replaced. The new series was designed to link in with the 'Leisure' map series. There were early problems however which caused annoying renumbering. In the following year the Secretary was invited to the map launch in Cornwall and presented with a complimentary set.

National Taxi Hotline

Reported at the time thus:- 'Very recently we heard of this service. We think it is important enough to draw it to your attention. We will be including the information in future editions of the Annual Guide. Many taxi operators subscribe to the "National Taxi Hotline" which works on a Freephone number 0800 654321.When you dial that number your call will be automatically routed through to the subscribing taxi operator nearest to your location and you have your taxi.'

National Trust Anniversary

The National Trust celebrated the hundredth anniversary of its first acquisition of a piece of coastal land. This was Barras Nose at Tintagel that was acquired by public subscription because of the threat of so-called coastal development, some of which is still very evident in Tintagel today.

You can look across from Tintagel Castle to Barras Nose the first coastal property ever acquired by the National Trust. There are the remains on the castle site of a Celtic monastery but Tintagel has no link to the mythical King Arthur but does to custard powder!

Farm Animals and You

David Squire wrote the following article for us – he is a farmer and represents the NFU on our Association Committee.

'As farmers we are asked many times about animal behaviour which can be alarming to walkers not familiar with them. Most importantly you can be sure that the farm animals you meet along the footpath are not a danger to the farmer, his family, or the general public, and if not teased, chased or interfered with, no harm will come to the walker.

'Generally speaking this means walking and strolling by them with a confident air. "Ah!" you may say, "what about cattle that follow me and my dog?"

Cattle by nature are very inquisitive and if feeling a little bored will walk, or worse gather speed, behind you. Personally I always carry a stick, and if they get too close (they follow us farmers as well), I turn and tell them to "GO AWAY". This has never failed, but you must be firm.

'Animals with young should never be interfered with. Sweet they may look, but the mother's instinct is to protect them, so best not to get too close. Sometimes you will meet animals directly on the footpath. A bit daunting if they are big, and here, if you are unable to move them, it would be prudent to walk off the path around them. Horses can kick and bite, so give them a wide berth.

'There is no magic formula, just common sense, but I truthfully say that in all the years my father and I have farmed I have never heard of any walker being injured by farm animals, either by walking through fields, or on the many miles of footpath that surround us. And go forth boldly, with a big stout walking stick, a friendly smile and greeting for us farmers, and enjoy your walking.'

Another farmer had this to say, that whilst working on his cliff top fields he took pleasure in seeing coastal walkers laden with packs along his section, but why did many ignore him? It would be nice to receive a friendly wave.

Dogs on Beaches

Despite our long term feeling that the coast path should always in fact be on the coast in a number of places it had been designated on beaches as an easy option. About this time more beach authorities were becoming health conscious and banning dogs from beaches particularly in the summer months. This gave a problem to walkers particularly those who were making a continuous journey. Which legislation took precedence – the statutory right of way that permitted dogs or the by-laws that banned them? We could only presume, from their failure to answer our Secretary's written questions, that many in local authorities did not then know either. It took a long time to sort this out, but eventually it became clear that with certain caveats, dogs could indeed cross the beaches if it is the designated route of the coast path.

Dartmoor Preservation Association

A mutual mail-out of our respective leaflets was arranged between the Dartmoor Preservation Association and our own. There was sufficient response to consider doing it again the following year.

Silver Jubilee Plans

Next year on May 5th 1998 it would be our Silver Jubilee. What should we do to mark the occasion? Andrew Bristow suggested walking the complete path in relays, and Mary Carter advocated massive press publicity. There appeared later to be problems caused by insurance considerations so that the walk in 1988 was not carried out. However, in the end, we decided to do something different – see next section below.

End of Path Markers

After discussions with the South West Coast Path Management Team a working party was set up to discuss end of path markers and how to bring them into being. It was said at first our Association would be the front-runners in the scheme but this largely proved not to be the case as horizons widened and costs particularly at the Dorset end of the path escalated. At the AGM in Truro our

Association launched an appeal for funds for the markers. Our Secretary's comment:- 'No doubt some of you will remember how disappointing it was on the day you finished the path to find nothing to photograph. Hopefully, there will be for those who come along in the future.' The Association launched a Silver Jubilee Appeal for end of path markers.

The position of the start marker at Minehead caused some dissension. The town council and our Association opted for a point on the coast opposite the present start of the coast path. The idea being that this was suitable now and still would be if we could get the routing along the sea front that we have so long requested. The South West Coast Path Team wanted a site nearer the railway station but eventually agreed. At the end at South Haven Point there were again disagreements about siting. One suggestion was even to put it in a car park! However, our Association was firmly of the opinion that it had to be at the end of the path. This did require planning permission discussions with the ferry company and agreement from the National Trust as well as investigation as to the suitability of foundation. There were the problems too that although all concerned seemed in favour, ideas became more grandiose and costs kept escalating. Eventually all these problems were overcome.

The Start of Path Marker, at Minehead, here it is only 630 miles (1014 Km) to the finish! Since it was erected, the most surprising outcome, has been the interest shown by all sorts of people, most of whom are never likely to attempt the whole path.

At Minehead the design chosen was that of an art student Sarah Ward: it was of a pair of hands holding a map. It was 'opened', if that is the right word, in February 2001 by Sarah Ward and Sir Ian Amory, Chairman of the South West Coast Path Forum. After its erection it certainly caused a lot of interest even from passers-by who had no knowledge whatsoever of the coast path!

The South Haven Point Marker was finally officially unveiled in the spring of 2003. It was designed by an artist David Mayne. The Secretary commented that the artist had 'created a floor compass two metres in diameter and a three metre mast fully rigged with steel sails with images that reflect the landscape, wildlife and heritage of the coast path corridor cut in the sails by laser. South West Coast Path Association members can also pat themselves on the back because your donations for the two markers amounted to £5350. Over the years if there is one thing that has come across really strongly from members, it was the lack of suitable memorials at each end. Those that completed the whole path felt extreme disappointment there was nothing to mark their own personal triumph. It is pleasing to have two markers we can all proudly stand beside with that triumphant grin.'

The Finish Marker, at South Haven Point at the entrance to Poole Harbour. All, who have completed the distance, will have memories for as long as they live.

Holywell, North Cornwall

Cornwall National Trust provided a new bridge across the back of the beach. This enabled walkers who did not wish to shop or stop to bypass the village on a more coastal route.

Mullion Cove

The Association, amongst others, successfully opposed the erection of a communications tower on the cliff above Mullion Cove. It had in fact been planned to have one foot of the tower straddling the coast path.

Mount Edgcumbe

Cornwall County Council proposed routing the coast path inland of the very pretty and attractive route through the orangery at the Mount Edgcumbe Estate. Our Association strongly objected to what we regarded as a retrograde move.

1998

South West Coast Path Project

In January an important meeting was held at the Secretary's home. Those present included Countryside Commission officers, the Chairman of the South West Coast Path Forum and members of South West Coast Path Team together with our own Chairman, Vice Chairman, Secretary and members of the Committee. 'The day was devoted to the future management of the coast path and how the Association sees its part in it. Also discussed was the part the Association will play in the implementation of the South West Coast Path Strategy and the Partnership. Never before have those responsible for funding and managing the trail travelled so far to meet us on our own ground.'

By the next year our Chairman Brian Panton was able to go on record. 'Very soon after the first meeting we thought we ought to inform all members of the group ... what this Association represents, our history, our aims and objectives. We created a document making all this very clear and it was rewarding to see that most of our aims, objectives and requirements for the future management of the coast path were incorporated into the Strategy published by the Steering Group in 1997. ... I foresee busy times ahead with even more responsibility and at the same time continuing our quest for a completed coast path. Being part of the Management Group does NOT mean that we lessen pressure on managers to fill the gaps and remove the path from roads.' Our Secretary, Eric Wallis was later to say of his work with them: 'whilst it is true we do not see eye to eye all the time with the path managers, it is also true that this group does accomplish much that is aimed at the well being and future hopes for the South West Coast Path'.

Look closely at the picture and you will see the walker has aged, but still, even after 25 years, the path is not finished!

Silver Jubilee Project

Our Secretary wrote this as our Association reached its Silver Jubilee year. 'Congratulations to us. We are 25 years old this year. Goodness me! Your Secretary whilst not a founder member back in 1973, did join the Association in 1975 and he can well remember the close-knit cosiness of the organisation in those days. Mrs D Lancey was the Membership Secretary when the membership was around 300. It is a fact that due to the persistent efforts of those members in those early days that we have got to where we are today.

'We are still an unrelenting pressure group as those in the County Councils, National Trust and Countryside Commission will verify. In spite of that we have developed an amicable relationship with them.

'From those early days when about 20 different authorities had their fingers in the coast path management pie and none consulted each other, we have now arrived at the South West Coast Path Partnership. ...We will continue to cause a fuss about this unfinished coast path. One wonders if it will be COMPLETED by 2023.'

Committee and Staff Changes

Two members of the Committee since its inception both stood down: these were Mary Carter and Derek Hexter the

Treasurer, both having given 25 years' service. There was regret but, as was stated then, can you really ask someone who has served that long to do more? Dennis Martin from Devon and Gareth Critchley from Cornwall also resigned from the Committee. We also lost our Membership Secretary Mary Macleod who had worked for us for no less than 18 years. Sarah Vincent of South Brent was later appointed in her place. David Richardson was elected to be the new Treasurer – he had a finance background and was familiar with the computerised accounting system we now had. He was also an active member of the Long Distance Walkers' Association.

Our Association decided to have an e-mail address. The Secretary's Report was renamed Annual Report. Joan Westaway a founder member and former Chairman said she 'had watched the Association grow and develop beyond the wildest dreams of those few original members in Newton Abbot in 1973'.

There was a discussion on the usefulness of organisations such as the Offa's Dyke Association and ourselves now path management services were strengthening. It was thought that no 'official' service could quite look at matters from the 'user' angle, which is what we are best at. Furthermore a partnership between the voluntary and public sectors fits the ethos of the day.

Eric said that the role of the Association Secretary was now becoming more 'political'. Most of the day-to-day work was going to paid assistance and that the title Administrator should come into being for the person doing this.

It was decided that the name of the Association should be changed from South West Way to South West Coast Path. However the old name would appear for a number of years to prevent any confusion as to who we were. There was some regret that our original simpler title had not been adopted but it was felt that the authorities would not come round to our point of view. In view of this we thought we would have to adapt our title.

Two other unusual forthcoming matters had the Committee's attention this year – the total eclipse of the sun in August 1999 and the Millennium in 2000. Undoubtedly the first would put a strain on accommodation because it was only in the extreme south-west that a sighting of a total eclipse would be possible. It was decided to put a warning in the Guide for next year. The worry about the Millennium was whether our computers might be affected. It was necessary to have these checked out.

When it came to the actual eclipse day many missed out because of cloud cover, although others were more fortunate. Few, however, will forget the incongruity of a brief night in the middle of day.

Putting the Coast Path Back on the Map

This was the title given to an exploratory venture to find out how much of the official path originally designated in 1952 was actually the walked route. It was decided to use the north Cornish coast, from Marsland Mouth to Land's End, as a trial sector. It was suspected, not without reason, that the actions of the sea would have altered some of the route. It had also become apparent that the authorities had not kept up with the paper work of varying the route where it had been improved. The task was to be performed by state of the art global positioning from satellites linked to the computer-based Ordnance Survey map. Path managers were invited to attend but our Association was refused any input on the grounds that it would make the job much slower.

The outcome of this first trial showed up so many discrepancies that it was deemed essential that the whole of the path should be tackled in the same way. This was done between May 1999 and February 2000. Ten kilometres were done each day walking an average of three days a week. The distances do not seem great but the survey took time and the equipment had to be carried all the time. It proved conclusively that the majority of the walked route did not have the statutory basis that it was supposed to do. In fact only 32% of the walked path was correctly aligned! Surprise, surprise, this new survey also threw up the conclusion that routes through towns were not adequately signed and the problem would have to be addressed.

For those who like such statistical information there was a plenitude, a little of which is reproduced here. 13% of what should have been a footpath was still on tarmac roads. 7% was not legally defined. 8% was admitted not to be on the best route. 5% of the path was not up to quality standards. On average eleven and a half kilometres of the path are subject to landslip each year and this problem is worst in Exmoor and Dorset. It was agreed that the length of the path had been underestimated and that all urban routes should be designated and signed. An annual emergency fund should be set up to prevent prolonged closures.

Access to Open Countryside

We received news of the Government's document *Access to Open Countryside*. This had been produced without any consultation with our Association but we decided we basically supported it and the need for a compulsory legislative approach. We also wanted cliffs and foreshores to be classified as open countryside.

EAGGF Bids

It was decided that we should apply for money from the European Agricultural Guidance and Guarantee Fund. This was a new departure for us because until now nearly all our funding had been from our members or grants from the Countryside Commission. The South West Coast Path Team was making an application for some 76 individual projects amounting to half a million pounds. Ours were included on a much more modest scale but it had not been appreciated at this stage how enormous was the amount of administrative work that would have to be done to obtain the grants. However, we did receive grants towards production of our path descriptions, IT equipment and funds towards new staff appointments.

Annual Award

Geoff Moore suggested at the AGM that the Association should consider making an annual award. This was to be to someone who was not a member of the Association but had made a significant contribution to the coast path. The first recipient in 1998 was Derek James who received a framed certificate and a piece of glassware. He had been the leader of the Plymouth team who worked hard to enhance the city waterfront walkway including the new path at Mount Batten Point and the off road section between Jennycliff and Bovisand. In 1999 it was awarded to Sue and Mervyn Venn of the Trevalsa Court Hotel, Polstreath, Mevagissey who had kindly donated a strip of their land to be utilised to reinstate the path after a landslide. Until this was done there was a long and most unsatisfactory diversion.

In 2000 the award went to the Sidmouth man Freddy Wedderburn, the Chairman of the Clifton Walkway Appeal Group and his group of volunteer helpers. This group initiated the idea of a coastal route from Western Beach

Mevagissey now makes the greater part of its living from tourists – once it was from pilchards. There are reports of 100 luggers working from here and mules used to move the quantities of fish. The fishwives, though, were said to be ruder than those at Billingsgate! Maybe surprisingly Mevagissey claims to be the first place in England to have its streets lit by electricity.

around the foot of the cliffs below Connaught Gardens to the end of Eastern Esplanade at Sidmouth. Until that time walkers had to use the pavement beside the busy road down from Peak Hill. This new path certainly provided a much-improved experience. 'See furher Sidmouth Clifton Walkway below'.

In 2001 the award again went to East Devon. There was a major rock fall at Seaton Hole, tons of rubble and boulders crashing down on the beach burying the flight of 97 steps. Not only did this deny access to the beach below but meant coast path walkers had additional road walking. East Devon District Council declined to do anything about it, on the grounds of cost. However, a retired builder Gordon Wellington was concerned to see people scrambling over the obstruction and put in a flight of steps very cheaply. The Council's reaction was to close these temporary steps on the advice of their insurance company!

Residents collected 5000 signatures for a petition to re-open the path. The Council then found a modest scheme to replace Gordon's steps and put others in their place, the whole job being done in seven days. We felt that Gordon's effort had undoubtedly led to the reinstatement of the coast path so he was awarded the Annual Award. Brian Panton awarded the certificate on site.

Our Annual Award in 2002 went to Chris Monk of Cornwall's Coast and Countryside Service who had at last completed the negotiations for the missing section of path between Downderry and Portwrinkle. In 2003 it was given to the army officer responsible for freeing the log-jam and permitting a coast path at Tregantle Fort when the ranges were not in use.

Porthoustock to Porthallow

This area had long been missing a coastal path. Surprisingly the northern half was an existing right of way that came to a dead end. The southern end was a disused quarry much used by locals for dog-walking. In between was a gap of fields. Our local Committee man Geoff Davis from Falmouth had worked hard to try and secure a realignment along the coast. He visited the area many times and established a rapport with the landowner. 'Between them they have agreed a beautiful path. You are not going to believe this but the landowner has received no contact from Cornwall County Council or the Countryside Commission for 2½ years. Incredible as it may seem, despite our continued pressure, the last we heard from those who determine what path you should or should not walk was from the Countryside Commission back in March 1996 when we were told negotiations were continuing. Geoff and the landowner have come to an agreement about a route, so why delay?'

Sidmouth Clifton Walkway

Terry Bound brought to our attention the projected footpath that would obviate walking by the road at the bottom of Peak Hill at Sidmouth. The idea was to construct a walkway below the cliff from Jacob's Ladder to the Town Beach. It was a Millennium scheme – public money had been promised but an appeal for funds was being made. The Association rather naturally looked favourably on the scheme.

Sidmouth was originally a fisher town it became a genteel resort. This process was aided by the lack of continental travel during the Napoleonic Wars. Later Queen Victoria stayed there whilst a princess.

1999

This year the Committee was much concerned with its Development Plan. Amongst other matters discussed were payment of subscriptions by standing order, and the possibility of using professional fundraisers and advertising for additional membership. Sarah Vincent, chosen from 98 applicants, was designated as Administrator and Liz Woollard became a part-time Publications Officer with specific responsibility for producing the Annual Guide. Both of these appointments were made with the aim of lightening the load on our Secretary. Another sign of the increasing amount of business was the decision to hold three committee meetings a year instead of two. We lost the services of Frederick White who had served on the Committee in various capacities for some twenty years. Although he had come comparatively late in life to walking, he had embraced it enthusiastically and put a lot back in the process.

Proposed New Countryside Bill

We were asked by the Department of the Environment, Transport and the Regions to make a submission on rights of way for consideration prior to the formulation of the new Countryside Bill. Our Chairman Brian Panton wrote the report that ran to no less than fourteen pages.

Internet

When news of this first featured, our Secretary wrote 'for those lucky enough to have the necessary facility'. Certain evidence there of how little we appreciated the future enormous growth of this new medium and how important it would become to our Association both for providing information and as a source of new membership.

What else was said at the time? 'South West Coast Path Association member Andrew Lack of the City University in London has created a multi-page site. It includes full details of the South West Coast Path together with full details of the Association and how to join, its publications and how to obtain them. There is a section for 'latest news' which is updated immediately information is received by the Association's Secretary about diversions and closures and re-routings etc. Its main delight is a Phototour that Andrew has spent many hours designing. This is a series of linked pages, each one with a photo and a tiny map showing where along the path the picture was taken. Navigation links are provided to step along the coast "towards Poole" or "towards Minehead" allowing people to "walk" the path. In addition to the individual pages there are "active maps" for each area, with clear red dots where photographs are available.'

Later for some years we discussed whether we should put information such as B & Bs on our website. The plus side was that more folk would have access to such information. The down side was that we might sell a lot less guides, which brought us in new membership, and that we would get no recompense for the time-consuming job of collating the information every year. Bluntly if people could get the information free why become a member unless you were highly altruistic? We therefore decided we would publish all the information on our website but it would be done securely so that only members could access that part of our site. Nevertheless at the Chairman's suggestion we conducted a straw poll at the AGM to see what percentage of our members were Internet users.

Safety along the Coast Path

By this time thoughts surfaced of how modern ideas of Health and Safety regulations might relate to our path. Whilst in no way did we wish to lure people into dangerous situations, on the other hand we did not want to see wild cliff land despoiled with ugly fencing. A legal case brought in Derbyshire happily made the point that users of cliff paths must take responsibility for their own welfare. Our Secretary put it this way: 'while the Association acts in the interests of coast path users, it nevertheless welcomes this judgement which it sees as a practical solution to using a coast path. Heaven forbid that the judgement had been in the reverse; would we have a 613 mile long 1.1 metre high balustrade for the safety of walkers erected along the edge of the entire South West Coast Path or danger notices every few yards? We want the coast path to remain, for the most part, a challenge and an adventure, particularly along the wilder stretches. So there you have it.'

Magazine Articles

An article written by Mary Carter on the coast path appeared in the *People's Friend*: this produced quite a response and permission was sought to use the article elsewhere for publicity purposes. *The Great Outdoors* in their December issue had an article about user groups concerned with National Trails. The Association was flattered to come out extremely well compared to others.

Porlock Weir was once written of as 'a spot made for peace and sweet do nothing'. As against that image is the fact, that once pit props were exported and small coal boats were still unloading here until 1948.

Overland Launch Lynton – Porlock Weir Re-enacted

A hundred years after this heroic feat it was re-enacted, this time of course on modern roads but there were ferocious winds and stinging rain. Andrew Bristow wrote this piece about the original event:

On 12 January 1899 the Lynmouth lifeboat received a call from Porlock to go to the aid of the Forrest Hall, a full-rigged ship of 3200 tons, anchored 1½ miles from Porlock and in danger of coming ashore because of a hurricane. The sea was breaking over the Esplanade and harbour at Lynmouth and it was impossible to launch the lifeboat Louisa and it was decided to haul the boat to Porlock Weir overland and launch it there. This was done in darkness leaving Lynmouth at about 8.30 pm using shire horses and the crewmen. They followed the exposed coach road to Porlock Weir where the Louisa was launched at 5.30 am. The Louisa escorted the Forrest Hall to Barry Roads in South Wales arriving at 5 pm.

Pendeen Watch lighthouse was built in 1900 after a series of shipwrecks hereabouts. Not far off in one direction is Boat Cove where an outdoor service is held every year on St Peter's Day, 29 June. In the other is an old 'Count House' the name for a one time mining office.

Count House at Botallack

The National Trust had bought this interesting building in 1985. It has now restored it and turned it into the local warden's office with an information point 'which explores the human and natural history of this fascinating coastal area'. Count house was the local name for a mine's office: perhaps the best known one to coast path walkers is the one close to Pendeen Watch.

2000

Ken Franey North Devon representative left the committee as did Don Millgate the Devon RA member. Ken Franey's position as North Devon representative was filled by Bryan Cath. Mike Farrell stood down as Merchandising Officer but stayed on as a Committee member. June Haywood of Torbay was a new recruit to the Committee. The Secretary said that he had heard that plans were being made to celebrate the 25th anniversary of completion of the path in 2003. In his opinion the coast path is very definitely not complete. He suggested the 25th anniversary of 'inauguration' would be better. He also mentioned that international interest in our path was growing as evinced by recent telephone calls he had had from: France, Jerusalem, Sardinia, Switzerland and the Yukon!

Sue Applegate of the South West Coast Path Team gave an illustrated talk on her recently completed condition survey of the whole coast path. She demonstrated the GPS equipment that she carried and explained how it was used and what will happen to the data when it is analysed.

Mark Owen, who subsequently replaced Sue, began re-surveying the path in 2002. This time it was to be more enlightened and was not to be a closet affair. Members of the Association were invited to attend and give their viewpoints on different sections of the path.

National Trails Trust

This was another pipe dream that never came to fruition that all the National Trails should be managed by an independent trust. Our Association feared that such a trust never would be allowed to be independent but always subject to the Countryside Agency. If that was to occur it would simply add another layer of bureaucracy to an already confused chain of command. However, as already stated it fell by the wayside but at the time a piece was written on how the path currently 'works'.

'Without the dedication of the many path managers dotted around the peninsula the Trail would not be half what it is today. It is staff from the Highway Authorities like Devon County Council or Exmoor National Park Authority, and the National Trust who manage the path on the ground with great commitment and enthusiasm. The result is a superb walking experience enjoyed by thousands every year. The coast path work is funded predominantly by the Countryside Agency, and as with other government bodies, allocation of annual budgets is undertaken at a high level. ... The annual South West Coast Path Forum which took place in Plymouth in June saw a gathering of about 80 representatives from around the region. The theme was signing and celebrating the path through its towns and villages – an issue, which incidentally we hope to address in the immediate future. The enthusiasm and interest at the Forum was wonderful. Gradually more and more organisations – the region's movers and shakers – are becoming aware of the coast path and its vital importance to the community and the local economy. ...We've come a long way since the early days of the Coast Path Project.'

Update of Youth Hostels

There are now 20 youth hostels along or close to the South West Coast Path. Hostels range from the 94-bed Georgian country house in Golant, through the 74-bed Victorian barracks inside 16th century Pendennis Castle, all the way to the little 25-bed hostel directly above the slipway at Boscastle Harbour. Prices are still reasonable except to those of long memory who once paid 1/6d. (7 1/2p.) a bed-night! A new hostel was opened on Portland situated just beyond the causeway in Castletown. It provides a link for those on the coast between Litton Cheney and Lulworth. In 2002 the new self-catering only 32-bed hostel, converted from the old Polbream Hotel, adjacent to the lighthouse, opened at the Lizard.

Mailing

We were able to reduce our postage bill considerably by opening an account with the Royal Mail and pre-sorting our mail-outs into postcode areas.

Glenthorne

The coast path at Glenthorne near County Gate suffered because a new owner of the property withdrew the agreement for a permissive path granted by the previous owner. Those in authority for many years have said that none of the coast path should be permissive but when push comes to shove they have seldom done anything about it. To be fair there is an argument on both sides but a loss such as this highlights the down side of using permissive paths.

Crock Point

A new path west of Lee Abbey around Crock Point in part compensated the loss of the better path at Glenthorne. This scenic new route reduced the amount of road walking in that area so it was doubly welcome. Our Secretary, Andrew Bristow and Bryan Cath attended. Eric Wallis wrote: 'it is an enormous improvement to the coast path. It gives splendid views both east and west. The latter, of course, makes us all the more conscious of what we are missing by not being able to walk the Duty Point section seaward of Lee Abbey ... Thank you Exmoor National Park.' The suggested origin of the name Crock is interesting. It is crock, as in the old name for earthenware pottery, and used here because clay was extracted in the 18th century and taken away to Holland by ship.

Ilfracombe, the chapel on the hilltop is dedicated to St Nicholas and is at least 600 years old; it was at one time used as a lighthouse. Kaiser Willhelm II is reputed to have attended school for a brief while in Ilfracombe, however bad the experience, surely not a sufficient reason for World War I!

Yeo Bridge Barnstaple

A new bridge close to the mouth of the river Yeo where it joins the Taw was built to replace the old railway bridge. This was on the one time Ilfracombe line that had been dismantled. This new bridge obviated the walk through the town and allowed pleasant progress along the riverside to cross the main road bridge over the Taw. It was mostly gain because it eliminated a devious back street detour to cross the Yeo on the bridge on the road out to Braunton. A few may have regrets because there are not many opportunities of passing a Marks & Spencer's on the path and no longer would one see the interesting Butcher's Row, a street reminiscent of medieval times with a predominance of one sort of retailer. The new bridge had to be a swing bridge to allow access of sand barges to Rolle Quay and was designed in an unusual inverted boat-shape.

Hartland Quay

The coast path was altered so that it descended to Hartland Quay. Originally for some unknown reason it had been kept inland from the Rocket House rejoining the coast south of the Quay. This was an obvious improvement that it made one wonder once again why those who originally drafted the route were seemingly so anxious not to adopt the best route. Having said that it must be admitted that long before the path was improved many a hungry, thirsty or weary walker had sought solace at the Quay on this magnificent but desolate stretch of coast!

2001

Foot and Mouth Epidemic

Like nearly all 'outdoor' organisations we suffered because of the Foot and Mouth epidemic. For many months all but the urban sections of our path were closed. Membership, instead of increasing as it had for many years, took a tumble. The sale of guides fell and we were left with some 800 unsold at the end of the season.

Our Secretary was kept busy on the telephone and sadly had this to say: 'I regret to say I had a few abusive calls blaming ME for the coast path closure! Goodness only knows what those at various County Halls and National Trust Regional Offices had to put up with. One of my callers aggressively informed me that the ban did not affect her as she was a vegan and she intended to continue walking on footpaths.' It became clear what an overall financial loss it must have been for the tourist trade. Just counting those cases known to our Association it added up to cancellation of 6500 bed-nights. Our website, which continually updated news of the crisis received no less than 10 000 hits during the period. One couple who had come all the way from Australia to walk the path were at Minehead to start on the day the news broke. Fortunately as they were on an extended tour, they turned tourists, Stratford, York etc and then came and walked the path when it reopened. Our Secretary had, however, been able to contact a member in Colorado USA the day before his intended departure to walk the whole path. Again it is pleasing to report this did not put them off, they simply delayed their departure.

O-Day

Thought was given to how we would mark the re-opening of paths when this came about. It was decided that the Association should try to redeem something from the disaster of Foot and Mouth by having a special day, O-Day. This was to remind the media and public of our work and to thank all path managers for re-opening the coast path so swiftly after the crisis. The problem was of course that although we knew it would come to pass it was impossible to predict in advance when the path would open.

The plan was to walk the whole of the path in a day, each walker wearing a symbolic square of green material. There was too at least one dog, Charlie, belonging to Jane Richardson of South Zeal, who walked that day with a green square around his neck. Eric Wallis estimated the whole path had, in fact, been walked in some six hours! Letters were sent to all Town Clerks on the route asking for their co-operation. Malcolm Appleton arranged a pre-event photo shoot. Bryan Cath walked from Combe Martin to Lee Bay and was met by the Mayor of Ilfracombe. Michael Coxson was met by the Mayor of Penzance. A pipe major who had led commandos ashore on D-Day in 1944 was photographed leading walkers at the start of the section Shaldon to Starcross.

The Admiral Benbow near the Quay in Penzance. Close to here tin was assayed at Coinage Hall This has nothing to do with money but refers to the coign or corner that was cut off the tin ingots for testing the purity of the tin.

Jurassic Coast

The East Devon and Dorset sections of our path were declared a World Heritage Site at the United Nations meeting at Helsinki in Finland in December. This gives them an equivalent status to such world famous natural wonders as the Great Barrier Reef and the Grand Canyon.

Personnel

We appointed Ken and Margaret Ward as the Association's Publicity Officers. Some of the longer-standing members will remember Ken Ward who with John Mason had been the authors of the *Letts Guides,* the first really useful guides to the coast path.

Colin Leigh and Bob Reid joined the Committee at the AGM.

Peddar's Way

The question is sometimes raised, is there any need for our Association, now that so much has been achieved? The days when no one looked at the path as a whole and one county did not know what was happening on the adjacent coast path, beyond their own boundaries, are thankfully far behind.

The Peddar's Way whose own 'Association' was wound up because the 'original objects appeared to have been achieved' provides a salutary warning. Waymarking was variable and in places non-existent. Routing was poor and long stretches of the path were either on tarmac roads or just beside them. Points of historical interest were by-passed.

On our South West Coast Path we have had and indeed continue to have just these sort of problems. We hope however by keeping a user's or customer's eye view on matters we can at least alleviate some and improve others. So we reckon that the Peddar's Way has convinced us that our Association still has a useful role to play and indeed without it, matters could easily become worse.

Great Ringstead windmill is passed on the Peddar's Way. On the coast path one-time water mills and the sites of tidal mills are more common.

Compliment from B & B

Our Secretary thought that as there were few letters from 'those that dry us off and feed us' that this one from Sonia and Peter Martin of St Ives should have a special prominence: 'we wrote ... to let you know that we have really enjoyed having walkers as bed and breakfast guests. They are no trouble and very interesting.' Our Secretary added how he wished some unsympathetic landowners could read that!

Minehead

The start of path marker was unveiled – see 'End of Path Markers' above.

Macmillan Way West

A new unofficial long distance footpath, but one with charitable intent, was opened from Castle Cary in Somerset to Barnstaple. Significantly they had problems in securing a route through Exmoor. This path was an offshoot of the main Macmillan Way that ran from Boston to Abbotsbury.

Mousehole

An improvement was made between Mousehole and Newlyn. An off-road combined cycle and walkway now separates walkers from the traffic where there is no pavement. This would not be an ideal solution in many places but those who have walked this particular stretch will appreciate what has been done.

Newlyn is the busiest commercial fishing port in Cornwall. At one time the Ordnance Survey determined sea levels here.

Poldhu

Geoff Davis reminded us that 2001 was the centenary year since Marconi had sent his first wireless signal across the Atlantic. Encouraged by a successful transmission of a signal from the Isle of Wight to Bass Point on the Lizard in January he proceeded to try out the much longer broadcast in December. His trial signal, this time from Poldhu, was picked up 2000 miles away in St John's, Newfoundland. Seven years later a full commercial transatlantic service was in operation. Furthermore a whole radio and television industry has grown up from these experiments to and from the coast path!

Slapton Sands

Devastating winter storms breached the A379 road where it was carried along the top of Slapton Sands. The route was not closed to walkers but as our Secretary said, 'those who have walked this before will be astounded at the amount of damage caused by the power of the sea'.

St Aldhelm's Head

Sir Bernard Lovell, astronomer of Jodrell Bank fame, came to Dorset to unveil a radar memorial on St Aldhelm's Head. The metal and stone memorial – comprising two miniature radar dishes and fire baskets – recall ancient and modern methods of invasion warning. Tony Viney said:- 'fires were lit to warn of the approach of the Spanish Armada and now we rely on radar. The memorial is a symbol of technical evolution in this country that has contributed so much to the safety of our country.'

This is the chapel on St Aldhelm's or St Alban's Head, it is called either. St Aldhelm was the first bishop of Sherborne, in Saxon times, when the diocese was important. The chapel has a rugged exterior but is well maintained internally and often decorated with flowers. There is a former coastguard row close by.

2002

Fifth Chairman

Bryan Cath was elected as our fifth chairman in place of Brian Panton who was standing down. Bryan thanked the members for voting him in as the new Chairman. He gave a brief resume of his career and his work on the Tarka Trail and as co-ordinator of the North Devon Walking Festival. He also outlined his vision for the Association's future. As Andrew Bristow did not wish to stand again, Brian Panton accepted the vice-chairmanship on a short term basis.

Other Changes

Our Publicity Officers Ken and Margaret Ward notified us they wished to withdraw. They had found their lack of IT skills a disadvantage. Geoff Davis from

Cornwall and Ann Richards the Dorset representative retired. Sarah Vincent our Administrator resigned to take up a full time job and Liz Wallis, our Secretary's wife, was appointed in her stead. This did initially give us some problems having two working ladies both Liz W, Liz Woollard being the other! However shortly the advantage of having all the administration under one roof showed tremendous benefits. Someone once said to Liz Woollard 'there's more to life than the South West Coast Path'. Her reply was 'is there? What's that then?' Liz Wallis went on record about a year in to the job 'What Eric and I are doing at Penquit means that thousands of walkers will have the holiday of a lifetime. There aren't too many jobs as good as this!'

After a lot of work we were able for the first time to accept credit card payments for merchandise and membership fees. This was obviously a sensible step, helping both our 'customers' and ourselves. The problem had been that for a relatively small organisation such as ours it was time-consuming and expensive to set up.

Direct Debits

The Association had for many years wished to introduce a system to enable members to pay by Direct Debit. In part this was caused by the complicated nature of the Standing Order procedure, for instance the Association would receive bank statements 32 pages long! Unfortunately at first the available schemes for Direct Debit were far too expensive for an organisation of our size. However eventually we found a package within our means so we now went ahead and implemented it. In 2003 our treasurer David Richardson reported that 20% of the membership was using the system. In the same way that Andrew Lack had helped the Association by setting up our website, Frank Lyon had skilfully adjusted our member's database to enable the transition to Direct Debits.

Videos, CD-ROMs and Television

Another aspect of modern technology and its usage was our offerings for sale of a CD-ROM of our website. Another CD was produced from the drawings of Sue Jeffreys. She had originally walked the path between 1994 and 1997 in four stages of approximately two weeks, drawing as she went. Not only did she draw places but also flowers. She had been good enough to let our Association use many of her drawings for illustrations in Newsletters and of course for the Completion Certificate. Carlton Television put out a series of programmes about some parts of the path but we thought it was unfortunate, that when there was so much relevant material available, they kept straying from the ambit of the path. Furthermore they adopted an irregular showing schedule which made viewing difficult.

Hartland Point Memorial

Northern Devon Coast and Countryside Service erected a memorial to the sinking in 1918 of the hospital ship *Glenart Castle* 20 miles off the coast of Hartland Point. Only 31 of the 186 men and women on board were saved. Hospital ships were painted white with large visible red crosses and showed full navigation lights during the hours of darkness and were, of course, unarmed. However they became a deliberate target of German U boats in the later stages of the First World War. Two other hospital ships were sunk off Cornwall.

Forrabury, south of Boscastle

Those who have walked the coast path hereabouts will have been sure to have noticed the ancient strip cultivation. This is sometimes called a stitch-meal system and the strips are referred to as stitches. The National Trust has been purchasing them for some time and this year managed to obtain the last two, making forty-one in all. The Trust manages the strips by ploughing them at least once every four years, an echo of an old rotational method of cultivation. This encourages certain special types of wild flowers. Another site close to the coast path where such a strip survival can be seen is at Braunton in North Devon.

Forrabury has one of the few survivals of the medieval strip system of cultivation though there is another at Braunton. To us, today, it seems a wasteful and time-consuming way to work. It did however ensure that everyone had an even distribution of the best and worst land in the parish. It is now all owned by the National Trust who attempt to cultivate it on a similar pattern to former times.

Studland

For a number of years we had hoped for an improvement to the coast path at Studland. Once again our idea was to get the path off the road and along by the sea. We were heartened when most of the land that would be required became the property of the National Trust. To our chagrin opposition to our ideas continued just as strongly. In fact so great was the resistance we even withdrew it from our wanted list thinking it might be impractical to obtain what we wanted. Then along came different personnel on the Trust's side and a splendid path was put in very quickly in two halves at slightly different times. The surprising thing was that the Trust never thought to sign their two halves as a continuous path. An incredible piece of not joined-up thinking! One of the assets of the new off-road path is that it passes the historically interesting Fort Henry.

2003

Jubilee Walk and other celebrations

The South West Coast Path Team decided to celebrate the year 2003 by publicising the fact that the South West Coast Path was now 25 years old. The event that prompted the celebration was that in 1978 the Somerset and North Devon section of the coast path was officially included into the coast path. We were in fact celebrating our 30th Anniversary, but organised our own Silver Jubilee walk as part of the proceedings.

Our Jubilee Walk took place on Easter Saturday, the 19 April. The basic idea was to walk the whole of the path in the day. The path was divided up into 70 sections and each guided group walk was limited to 15 people. Our Secretary had advertised it thus:- 'Whether you are in London, Liverpool or Lincoln come and join us. Let's try to make this the longest and best attended walk ever, in one day'.

The actually celebration was similar to O-Day in that we arranged to have each section of the coast path walked on a single day by asking for volunteer guide/leaders. There were two principal differences; firstly this time we would walk the other way round or as we would have it 'backwards'. The second was that we could fix the date long in advance which made it much easier for all concerned. It was decided that Easter Saturday would be suitable and one likely to attract a good turn-out. The problem with O-Day had been that we had no

The Ladies Window is a striking feature of the North Cornish coast near Trevalga a few miles beyond Boscastle. Incredibly the path was routed so that many walkers missed it. We have requested a few yards change of route. The intrepid can pass through the arch and picnic on a ledge but take care not to drop your lunch, you will not be able to retrieve it!

idea when the path would be re-opened therefore we could not designate a specific day for the walk. A special discount of 20% on a first year's subscription was to be offered to new members joining as a recruiting drive.

As customary our Secretary came up after the walks with some interesting information. Of the 668 participants, there were two six-year olds and one nine-year old. By taking part three members actually achieved completions of the whole South West Coast Path. 43 students from Plymouth English Language School walked. They came from Japan, China, Russia, Liechtenstein, Australia, Germany, USA, Romania, Switzerland, Austria, Hungary, Ukraine and France. In fact all the world's continents except South America and Antarctica were represented. Well over 100 walkers came from outside the west country and stayed a total of 415 bed nights. There were several dogs who walked on Easter Saturday and it is reported that one was called 'Eric'. One leader, Malcolm Appleton reported, 'the only difficulty was the fact that the pub at Porlock Weir was closed when we arrived!'

The South West Coast Path Team co-ordinated other events and activities during the year organised by Coast and Countryside services, the National Trust, BTCV and the RSPB. Artists, musicians, writers, poets and photographers were encouraged to produce work that used the coast path as inspiration. Local organisations such as parishes and Women's Institutes were invited to get involved in one way or another.

English Heritage

A coast path historical environment project was set in train by English Heritage. The South West Coast Path Team would be involved. If this is well done it should be a fascinating project indeed because there are certainly items of historic interest ranging from the Bronze Age up to the Second World War along the route of the coast path. For those with an interest in such things not only can you walk over 600 miles but pass by evidence of three millennia.

Clavell Tower, Kimmeridge Bay

This Landmark Trust owned observatory or folly was in danger of being undermined because of coastal erosion. It was therefore proposed that it should be taken down and moved further inland. The Landmark Trust opened an appeal for funds to do this.

Clavell Tower, near Kimmeridge, is being undermined by the sea and it is hoped to move it further inland. The Rev. John Richards Clavell built it around 1820 but there is controversy whether it was built as an observatory or a folly.

Chapter 8

Footpath Information Sheet (Later Annual Guide)

The very first edition of this went out in July 1973 with apologies for it being such a rush job but with the hope to improve in future. It was a duplicated document with 12 pages and an introductory cover. This stated as follows:-

The South West Way is in various stages of development. In places miles of it are well trodden, cleared, stiled and even signposted. In other places, no right of way exists at all and even if it does it is certainly no guarantee that progress is possible!

Quite frankly the only hope an intending walker has of walking long stretches without difficulty is to subscribe to our maps which are not available yet. (See 'Maps'.)

However, please do not let us deter people from trying. We think we have a magnificent walk in course of preparation – the more it is used, the sooner it will be completed!

We regard it as one of our functions to supply useful information, to help people use 'The South West Way'. Suggestions for improving this information sheet are welcome.'

Accommodation took up six pages but as yet there were no facilities listed and telephone exchanges were place names, not the numeric codes of today. They were however listed in path order from the very start. There were some 130 addresses (661 entries 2005 Guide). There was a page on 'Books', a page on 'British Rail', two pages on 'Bus Services', a page on 'Ferries' and a page on 'Maps'. The book page is dismissive about the only two books available covering the whole path. 'Neither of these books ... is, in our opinion totally satisfactory. They provide much useful information but some of it is out of date. They do not measure up in usefulness to the best type of walker's guide available in the Lake District or Pennines.' British Rail then had a service Maiden Newton to Bridport that has since ceased. Devon General has disappeared as a bus operator. Ferries were included then as now, but we also mentioned two one-time ferries which were no longer available; these were Hayle/Lelant and Dawlish Warren/Exmouth. The maps listed were 1" and 2½" and the latter were only available for some areas. We hoped to sell these Information Sheets at 5p. (The 2005 Guide costs £7.00 but is decidedly larger at 176 pages compared to the original 12!).

The idea gained acceptance and by 1975 just two years and two editions on there were two new sections; 'Other Useful Addresses' and the far more important 'State of the Path'. This was a brief report on sections of the path all the way from start to finish. In 1976 the name 'Footpath Information Sheets' was

South West Coastal Path

A COMPLETE GUIDE
1976

First illustrated Guide cover in 1976, Peter Carter with high-pack looking at St Michael's Mount. The Mount in earlier times was a monastery, after the Reformation it belonged to the King; it then became a private house and latterly National Trust. It is an island at high tide.

jettisoned in favour of 'A Complete Guide'. The cover was a different colour, yellow, and there was an illustration of a walker with a high-pack, our son Peter, looking at St Michael's Mount. It was drawn by, and donated to, the Association by Mark Richards who kindly did this for a number of years. In 1976 we introduced for the first time a measurement in miles and kilometres for every section. We also introduced our first Grading System though as we said in the introduction we found it a rather invidious task. We also added of our 'severe' grading 'we have taken lack of escape routes, distances from public transport etc. a little into our consideration. It is not purely a question of physical difficulty.' Later in 1985 we modified this grading to be only based on purely physical difficulty. In 1976 our sales reached 500 and we stepped up our order for 1977 to 600: our Guide in 1977 had a pink cover and incorporated 'An Invitation to Membership'.

The Guides at this stage were A4 which was not a convenient size to carry in a pack so from 1978 onwards they were reduced to a smaller A5 format but the 32 pages of 1977 became 40 pages of smaller print in 1978. Guides were now first printed rather than just duplicated.

This year saw a 'History' section for the first time. It had the introduction that follows: 'we are sometimes asked what we have done? Fair question? Set out below are some of the main things in which we have been involved one way and another. Let us say as well, we send a steady flow of reports on path deficiencies to the authorities concerned and we continually nag the Countryside Commission to try and get some action from them. This is perhaps the most important, but so far the most unproductive part of our work!'

Although we had included some assistance to campers before, it was not until 1980 that we started to list actual 'Campsite' addresses (152 were entered in 2005). In 1980 we also issued our advice for walkers tackling a long distance footpath for the first time; it was headed 'A Word to Beginners'. It features today but is under the heading 'Long Distance Walking Advice'. Another short but continuing feature was started in 1980 which was 'Weather'. Our introduction then was: 'No, we offer no advice or predictions on this subject, to do so would only include us in the ranks of those who are wrong!'

From 1981 at the suggestion of Tony Collings it was decided that every member should get a free Guide. That year there was a considerable improvement in the format. All sections now ended at places accessible by road, and towns and villages were listed showing those that had rail facilities and the OS map for that section. In 1982 we added a possible way to break up the path to help people walk it in convenient sections under 'Itinerary – suggested'. This took quite a lot of thought because as well as trying to balance the effort required, each section had to begin and end at a place well served by public transport. By 1983 prosperity must have been on the increase as we mentioned 'Taxis' for the first time and the price of the Guide had risen to £1. In 1986 we adopted a new format and presentation; the old matt finished cover, with drawn illustrations, gave way to a glossy one with a colour photograph. The first used was of Start Point but over the years a number of other highlights of the path were depicted, such as Damehole Point (north of Hartland Quay),

Kynance Cove, Polperro, the Mewstone off Wembury, Golden Cap, and Old Harry Rocks.

In 1994 it was decided to make reference to the relevant Path Description available in the trail description section of the Guide. In 1996 improvements were made to the information in the Accommodation Section. In 1997 it was decided that in future all references to the old Pathfinder maps would be removed in favour of the new Explorer maps. In 1998 there was a considerable problem when the printer producing the Guide went into liquidation. Fortunately Mary Macleod had a back-up copy so she was able to get it printed elsewhere. In 1998 the title became 'The South West Coast Path 1998 Guide' instead of the old title 'The South West Way'. This title, with the appropriate year, has continued.

Polperro in its busier fishing days was once known as 'Polstink'. What caused the worst smell was the use of fish that had gone bad as fertilizer on the local fields!

In 2000 Tourist Information Centres were listed. We also added two new categories of information to our Accommodation section. These were Kit Transfer (KT) which meant the accommodation provider was willing to transfer your kit to your next accommodation address and Pick up and Drop (PD) which indicated a willingness to pick you up from the coast path nearby and drop you back there the next morning.

In 2002 we introduced 'Section Timings'. We had been asked for these several times but had always fought shy of offering them because of the difficulty of getting comparability. However, we now thought, by using existing work in Cornwall and using it as a standard, we could expand this coverage to the rest of the path. Times were done overall for the official path, not sadly our suggested alternatives, and did not allow for refreshment or other stops. We were conscious too that so many factors can affect one's speed; for instance the weather, the amount you are carrying and the interest of the section. What we were aiming at was a fair average. However, as long as the times were comparable, once a walker had done one or two sections and related their times with ours they could soon extrapolate their likely time for any other section. 2002 was also remarkable in that, for the first time, we had to have a reprint: the poor sales of 2001 caused by the Foot and Mouth epidemic had made us overcautious in our initial order.

In 2003 we incorporated an application for membership form. Why ever did we take so long to think about this? We had had an invitation before but no easily used coupon.

Towards the end of the Guide we say this, it is apposite so pardon the repetition. 'Alfred Wainwright at the end of his work on the Pennine Way said "you have completed a mission and achieved an ambition. You have walked the Pennine Way, as you dreamed of doing. This will be a very satisfying moment in your life. You will be tired and hungry and travel stained. But you will feel great". Dear reader, just substitute the South West Coast Path for the Pennine Way. We will add whether you have been lucky enough to walk the whole way from Minehead in one go, or simply as most of us have, in bits and pieces over a period, nonetheless you will be glad you walked and have just finished Britain's longest and finest footpath. It's a longer step than most take in their lifetime!'

Valley of Rocks – *The start of the path from Lynton is spectacular. First there is the engineered North Walk, 400 feet high above the sea, cut in the early 19th century, and then one enters the Valley of Rocks. There have been considerable arguments about the valley's geological origins but this need not prevent your enjoyment.*

Sheep's eye-view – *The sheep are obviously interested in the walker, but we are spared their opinions!*

Traditional Clovelly – *Clovelly's main street is cobbled steps unsuitable for wheeled traffic. Donkeys were the traditional means of transport. Here the animals wait to carry up the luggage from guests staying at the New Inn.*

Angel's Wings – *Is an unusual summerhouse, of uncertain date, built for the Hamlyn family of Clovelly Court. It has been suggested that the spot chosen was to enable the wife of one of the Hamlyns to look in the direction that her daughter Charlotte, had gone on marriage to Sir Arthur Chichester. The Clovelly estate was owned for several centuries by the Cary family, it was then taken over by the Hamlyns. They were bankers who purchased a north Devon estate just as the Barings bought theirs in south Devon at Revelstoke.*

Damehole Point – *This view looks north from Hartland Quay to Damehole Point and Lundy Island in the distance. This stretch has been well named the 'Iron Coast'. There is a definitive right of way out on to Damehole Point possibly the most dramatic in England, which has now sadly eroded. Lundy is of Norse origin, which is unusual for a Devon place-name; it means puffin island.*

Porthcurno Beach – *Porthcurno has more than one reason to be remembered. It was once a main landfall for submarine cables and had the Cable & Wireless technical school. It now has a good museum to remind one of its great days as a communication centre. It is also the home of the Minack outdoor theatre.*

Loe Bar – *The coast path crosses Loe Bar a sandy beach that separates the sea from Loe Pool. Loe Pool is the biggest natural lake in Cornwall. Close by is a memorial to the men of HMS Anson. It was wrecked here in 1807 with considerable loss of life. Henry Trengrouse watched the tragedy, pondered on it and came up with the idea of the rocket life-saving apparatus. It has since saved thousands of lives, but it cost Henry a fortune to develop; he was poorly rewarded and died in poverty.*

Cadgwith – *Cadgwith is a most attractive Cornish fishing village. Close by to the south is the Devil's Frying Pan, a collapsed cave. A little to the north is Poltesco where there are the remains of an old serpentine factory. In its Victorian heyday when the rock was much in demand for fireplaces and shop-fronts they even had a showroom in The Strand in London.*

St Mawes Castle – *St Mawes Castle was one of a chain of early artillery castles built on the orders of King Henry VIII. Only once did it see action, this was towards the end of the Civil War in 1646. It surrendered in short order, a great contrast to Pendennis Castle close by at Falmouth that put up a sturdy and prolonged defence.*

Rame Head – *Rame Head in the distance is a dramatic headland to the west of Plymouth with a long and interesting history. It was a fort in Iron Age times and had a medieval chapel to St Michael. There is a record as early as 1543 of a watchman paid 8d to look out for ships returning from the Newfoundland cod trade. It had a beacon at the time of the Armada and defences in World War II. The picture is taken from the grotto built for Princess Adelaide who later married King William IV.*

Golden Cap – *The highest point on the mainland south coast of England. One needs to see it late on a sunny day to see it at its golden best. There was a prehistoric settlement on the top.*

Chesil Beach – *The view north westwards from Portland along the Chesil Beach. To the right of the picture are Portland Harbour and Weymouth. Portland is always called an island though in truth it is not. The Beach is over 17 miles in length of which some 12 miles has water on both sides. It is an alternative that indeed makes a tough unremitting pebbly walk.*

Durdle Door – *Durdle Door is one of the best known of many natural arches along the coast path. They were created by the sea. The action of the waves on the cliffs formed them, and surely in time they will also be destroyed by the sea. The once famous arch at Corbyn Head, Torquay, has long since been eroded away.*

Tilly Whim Caves – *Tilly Whim Caves is a misnomer, these caves were originally quarrymen's tunnels. Whim was a device for lowering stone to the waiting boats below. The quarries were worked for centuries indeed men went from here to join Monmouth's ill-fated revolt in 1685. Now all quarrying has ceased and the nearby area has become popular with climbers. The 'caves' were once open to the public but now with their immediate surroundings are reserved for bats and birds.*

Old Harry Rocks – *When you reach here you have not far to go; Studland the last settlement on the path is only a mile away. Old Harry and Old Harry's Wife are rock stacks of harder chalk. They are from the same band of rock as the Needles on the Isle of Wight.*

Brownsea Island – *Sunset at the end of the path South Haven Point. Brownsea Island in Poole Harbour was the scene of Baden Powell's first ever Boy Scout camp. The island is still one of the few places that our native red squirrel may still be found.*

Chapter 9

Path Descriptions

We realised at a very early date that there was scope for more detailed descriptions for short stretches of the path. Our particular thought was that as well as describing the actual path they should include items of interest that one passed on the way, famous people associated with that particular piece of path and other miscellaneous information. We also hoped to give relevant information about access so that a particular stretch could be tackled as a 'day walk'.

The very first Description is dated 1/10/74, was 'Bigbury-on-Sea to Salcombe' and was a joint effort by the Chairman and Secretary to try and work out our formative ideas in practice. There have been changes since the early descriptions were written so maybe some future historian will use them to get an update on the area at that particular time. For instance two coastguard cottages were still used by them at Hope and there was then a coastguard lookout on Bolt Tail. A few quotations may give the flavour: 'Bigbury-on-Sea has little to recommend itself to the walker but it is a very popular and often overcrowded venue for the day tripper, with a fine beach particularly suitable for children.' 'Upon this stretch of path is Beacon Point which is said to be the point from which the first sighting of the Spanish Armada in Devon was made, and upon this point the first of the long chain of Armada beacons was lit.'

To see Inner Hope you have to make a detour, of at least a hundred yards, from the coast path, but it is worth it! Perhaps the most surprising thing about the place is the fact that there was once a cinema here, called appropriately The Barn.

'The path now passes Starehole Bay, and although it was at the Ham Stone that the Herzogin Cecilie received her death-blow, her last resting place is beneath the waters of Starehole Bay. She was the last of the great sailing grain carriers, and she was as stubborn in her dying as she had been steadfast in her living.'

Path Descriptions at this juncture and for some while to come were sent out free to members with Newsletters as an extra incentive to join. They were additionally sold at a small charge. The second Description was only brief, not two full pages and was 'Salcombe to Torcross', which came out in January 1975. Beesands then had a pub and two shops, and 'an extremely visually intrusive caravan site'. *The Cricket Inn* has survived but both shops have long gone, as did the caravan site in 1991.

Torcross was part of the battle training area prior to the 'D' Day landings in Normandy. All local inhabitants were evacuated. The American Sherman Tank was dredged up from the seabed and is a stark reminder of the heavy casualties incurred when German e-boats wreaked havoc on practising laden landing craft.

A G (Tony) Collings contributed a series of early Descriptions, for instance 'Treryn Dinas to Mousehole', 'Place Manor to Mevagissey' – 'While no part of Cornwall's Southern Coastline can be said to be off the tourist track any more, this section must be the closest approximation in an age of mass mobility' and 'The Purbeck Coast – Kimmeridge to South Haven Point'. The Association was very fortunate to have these and later contributions from Tony because he was not only a keen amateur naturalist but was also a skilled researcher so that he was able to impart a great deal of information he had found about the specific areas. Tony Collings also produced two historical descriptions. The first of these was called 'The South West Way 125 Years Ago', and described a journey made by Walter White in 1854. They were later incorporated in 'The South West Coast Path National Trail – A History'. This was worked on in 1998 and had a general write-up on the origins of the path as well as the two specific earlier studies.

Bryan Williams, an enthusiastic early member, wrote 'Brixham to Labrador Bay'. He was a professional railwayman so not surprisingly the Broadsands viaducts are mentioned and the Torbay Steam Railway whose steam locomotives 'are resplendent in the authentic GWR lined Brunswick green livery, with gleaming brass and copperwork, and the carriages are painted in the Great Western's chocolate-and-cream livery'. Bryan also provided the 'Railway' information for our early Footpath Information Sheets.

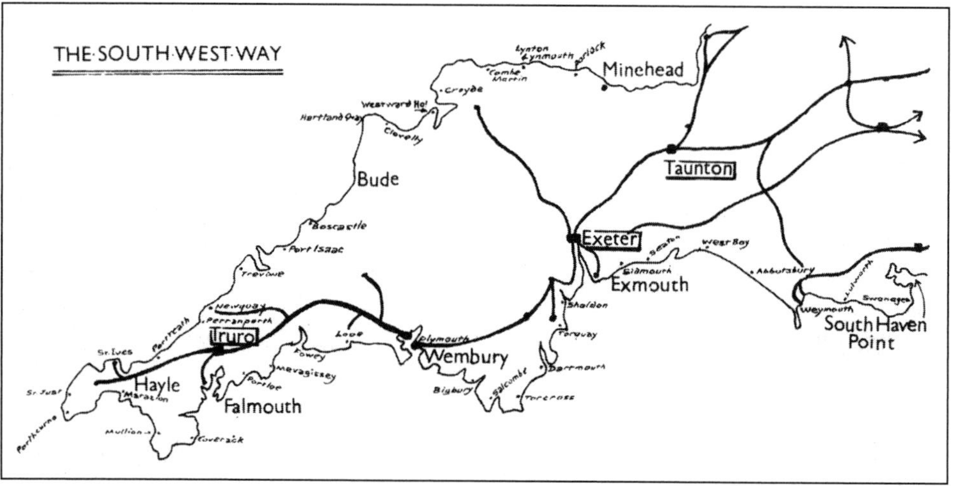

Rail map provided for us by Bryan Williams a keen walker and professional railwayman.

In 1977 out came 'Hartland Point to Marsland Mouth (The Iron Coast)'. 'There are so many good parts of the coast path that it is sometimes invidious to try and make comparisons. I can only say as a Devonian born and bred, that to me this is the most exciting part in all Devon! If this is not good enough for you, consider Hoskins' comments on this area "it contains the most impressive cliff scenery in England and Wales"'. Soon followed Denis Newson's 'The Coast Path within the Exmoor National Park, part 1, Minehead to Lynmouth'. 'Its grandeur emanates from the high hog's back cliffs which are different from the usual flat topped variety found in most other parts of England'. Another early Description was Harry Reddaway's 'Through the Lulworth Ranges'. Later the descriptions were tied in to start and finish at our standard section points.

Maps and illustrations began to feature in the descriptions of North Cornwall thanks to Mark Richards. Others also helped with the mapping – the authors of the *Letts Guides*, Ken Ward and John Mason, kindly consented to using theirs. Brian Panton contributed some very clear maps. Actual photographs were also reproduced. In 1986 it was decided to review the whole path with the idea of preparing a future grid or skeleton to cover all the remaining areas that had not yet got descriptions. 'These have grown up a little haphazardly over the years and our long term aim is to have standardised descriptions of approximately the same length of path all with maps and all illustrated'. By 1988 there were still 15 descriptions needed to complete the 'grid'. We were issuing 2 a year which would take seven and a half years and wondered if it could be stepped up to issuing 4 to speed the job.

By 1995 we had this to say:- 'The Path Description issued with this Newsletter is the Dorset Inland Route written by Ann Richards and Brian Panton. Members will realise that there now remains just one to do for completion of the whole path. We refer of course to Torcross to Dartmouth. Due to circumstances that are well known we have avoided it until a decision is made about Devon's non-coast path between Strete Gate and Warren Point.' However as matters became more protracted, the unsatisfactory non-coast route was written up by Frederick White and issued in the spring of 1996. This completed the task of producing a Description for every original section. (Portland was to follow, but it had not been envisaged as part of the coast path originally.)

This is the lighthouse at Portland Bill on the southern tip of the 'island'. Portland's main industry was, for centuries, quarrying, but its relative importance has declined. Note the derrick in the picture. The most famous building to use the stone was St Paul's Cathedral in London. Sir Christopher Wren came in person to familiarise himself with the stone's extraction.

Frederick in the introduction of his description wrote this:- 'This section of the coast path contains some excellent scenery and considerable interest along parts of the route. Sadly this section also contains a five-mile stretch which is considered by the Association and others to be the worst part of the whole of the 600-plus miles of the South West Way.'

In 1995 it had been decided that Path Descriptions should be produced on a uniform basis, and that lengths should accord with the sections given in the Annual Guide. A scheme was drawn up to effect this. It was decided that Path Descriptions should contain about 50% description/information and 50% history/flora/fauna/geology etc.

The description which really completed the set came out in 1996; this was Portland, still not part of the coast path then but the route given was all on legal rights of way. It was written by John Chaffey and had useful maps and good photographic illustrations. It started on an optimistic note:- 'Although this circuit of the Isle of Portland is at the moment optional, it is soon likely to become part of the official South West Coast Path National Trail. The Isle of Portland is unlike the rest of Dorset and it is the very difference that makes the circuit so rewarding.'

There was for a while discussions on how estuarine routes should be handled. Should we have a separate description including these? But in the end it was decided that each estuary route should be incorporated in the relevant description. In 1999 we set out on a policy of revision and standardisation offering a 'January sale' of old stock.

Thanks to modern computer techniques the problems of print-run lengths and keeping descriptions up to date have largely been solved. A complete set for the whole path is now available. Our thanks to all those who have contributed to this work, but possibly all those involved would readily admit they learnt more about the path in the process.

Chapter 10

Books

Over the years we gave help to a number of authors who produced guidebooks to the coast path. The first of these was Mark Richards' *Walking the North Cornwall Coast Path.* Mark Richards was a protégé of Wainwright and Mark's Cornish book mirrored that man's famous style with maps and illustrations. Mr G H Osborn wrote a book *South West Way Walks* (Part 1 Lyme Regis to Poole) and very generously donated the proceeds and copyright to our Association.

The most significant early co-operation was the help given to Ken Ward and John Mason to produce their set of three *Letts Guides* for the whole path. They came to our home on a wintry day and took up the whole dining table with their maps and manuscript so that the lunch of steak and kidney pudding had to be served in the kitchen! They had heard of us originally by picking up one of our handout cards in Portloe.

The *Letts Guides* were undoubtedly the first set of effective guidebooks to the whole path. They were produced in three volumes; No 1 was Minehead to St Ives, No 2 St Ives to Plymouth and No 3 Plymouth to Poole. The format was a map page facing a relevant page of text; this is something that even the modern National Trail Guides have failed to achieve. *Letts* did include in their Introduction 'Although originally mooted some twenty years ago the path remains very much in a development state. Certain sections have been impeccably waymarked and cleared, other stretches are unmarked and overgrown.' The *Letts Guides* sold so well that that only two years later in 1979 we were assisting them with an updated second edition. Even the second edition had its faults but as we said:- 'it is in our opinion the best buy of guides of the whole path presently available'.

We next helped Brian le Messurier with his *South Devon Coast Path Guide* (1980). It was still all very informal – he came to tea and we then had a working evening. The Guides were originally HMSO publications published for the Countryside Commission. The ones first produced were very poor indeed with masses of extraneous matter and not enough information about the path. 'Whilst we would be the first to agree that interest is one of the great features of Long Distance Footpath walking, those who buy a guide to a path have the right to expect that the path itself should be the priority.' ... 'We will still hope that the Official Guides will get even better, particularly the maps, but we can recommend this book which is a lot more than you can say for the first of them.'

These HMSO guides were later developed into the National Trail Guide Series. Aurum Press approached us in 1987 to ask for help in producing them although at that stage they had no authors lined up. Our Committee agreed to give 'as much help as possible in the production of these books'. This new series would not be limited to county boundaries but run from estuary to estuary. They proposed to call them all *South West Coast Path* and there would be four books; Minehead to Padstow; Padstow to Falmouth; Falmouth to Exmouth and Exmouth to Poole. The first came out in 1989, the remainder in 1990. Our Secretary wrote of them:- 'These are very good books and with one in your pocket plus our Annual Guide for accommodation, tide tables, up to date path information and detailed walking routes around rivers, the coast path explorer will be well served'. By 1994 they were working on new editions. Most but not all the errors in the first editions were corrected. They are undoubtedly the best set of guides available but either by lack of attention to detail or cheese-paring on costs they are not flawless.

In 1983 Peter Dawson's *The South West Way – A Traveller's Companion* was published. This 'was the first book written on the entire path clockwise and the first book to write up items of interest the whole way round the path'.

A book came out in 1985 as the first of a series this was *Along the South West Way* Part 1 Minehead to Bude. This was by A G (Tony) Collings, who had kindly written many of early Path Descriptions, and it was a well-informed description of the path with a lot of information about places along the way. It also had an interesting introductory history of the path. Sadly it did not prove a commercial success so that the other volumes never appeared.

In 1986 the most humorous book written about the South West Way appeared in print: *500 Mile Walkies* by Mark Wallington. 'This book tells the story of two city slickers (one four-legged, one two) coming to terms with the countryside on a journey along Britain's longest continuous footpath, from Somerset down the coasts of Devon and Cornwall to Dorset. The four-legged walker was Boogie, a mongrel more used to travelling on London transport and the author offers shrewd observations of people, seascape and countryside along the South West Way in humorous style.' Whatever the previous experience of the dog it is quite obvious that the author knows more about walking than he admits. Nonetheless it still remains the wittiest book yet on the coast path.

This is Rowan who with his boss Kim Parker completed the path. What is more he did it the hard way carrying his own 'woofsack'!

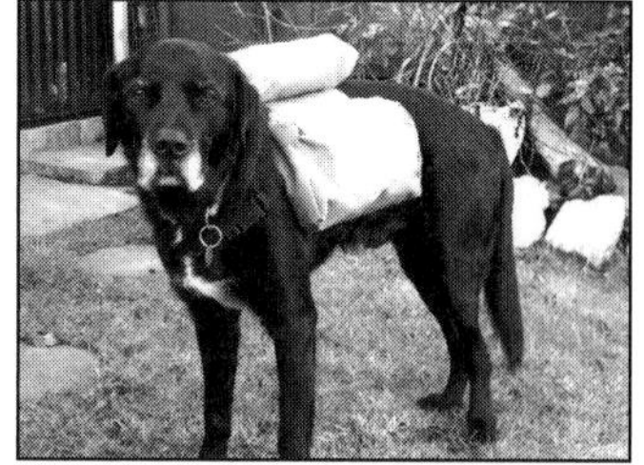

It is not exactly a book but maybe this is the place to mention it. In 1994 the Association became deeply involved with a London company making a video of the South West Way. They had already produced them for the Coast to Coast Path and the Pennine Way. We made suggestions as to what we considered were the most scenic and varied sections. The Secretary said:- 'The South West Way end to end from your armchair – now that has to be a Christmas present'.

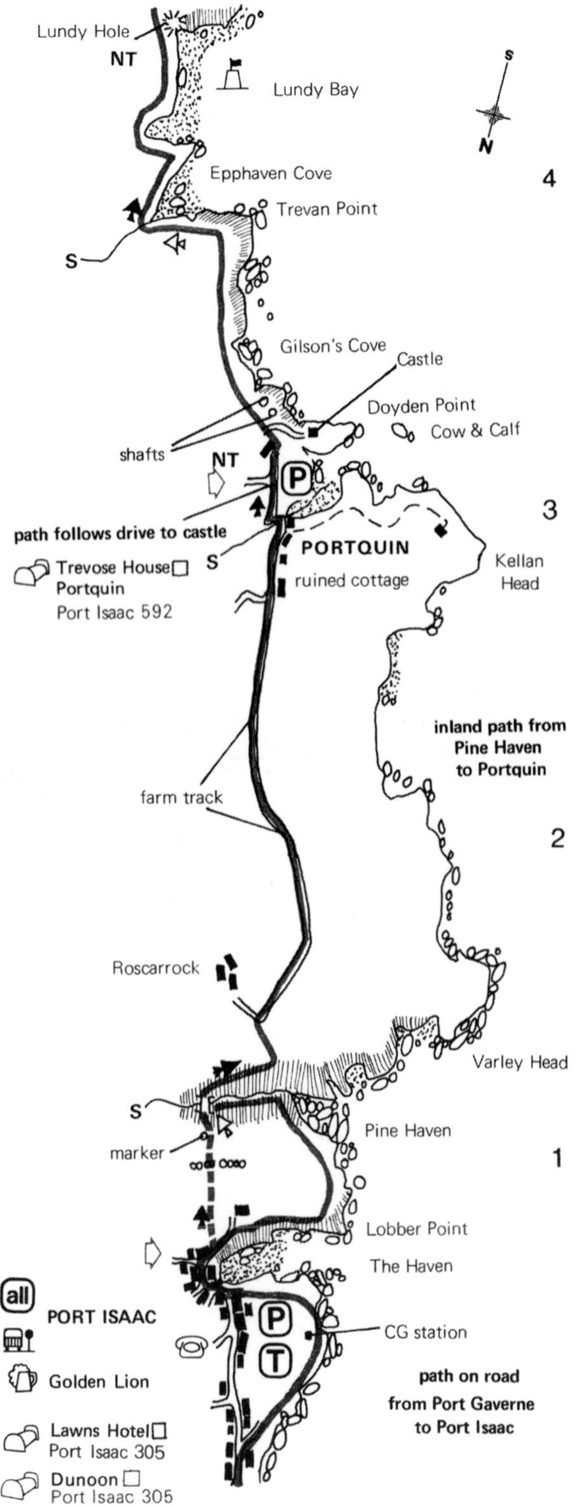

29. Port Gaverne-Port Isaac-Lundy Bay

4¾ miles 7¾km From Minehead 121¾ miles 195km

Going: the Path follows the road for ½ mile to Port Isaac and then due to an obstruction on the coast, is diverted inland to Portquin. From there a pleasant cliff path to Lundy Bay.

Port Isaac is only a few minutes up the road from Port Gaverne.

Port Isaac (from the Cornish for 'corn port') is one of the most picturesque of Cornish fishing villages. Its small quay, built in the 15th century, is no longer so busy with fishing boats but round the harbour the old houses look much the same as in the old days. The narrow streets and passages, one only 1½ft wide, 'Squeezibelly Ally', always delight the visitor.

Follow the 'public footpath' sign which stands at the foot of the narrow street which climbs out of the little town on the south side of the Harbour. From there the Path is well signposted all the way to Portquin, rounding Lobber Point before crossing the stream by a footbridge. It then turns inland passing close to the farm of Rosscarrock, parts of which are said to be 12th century, and continues across the fields, eventually coming out on the road just above Portquin. The field path tends to get very muddy in wet weather.

A few yards down the road on the right is the ivy-covered ruin of a small house. Inside you can see how it has been built of local slate, using also the rock for a wall. Portquin has a few cottages and a long derelict building once used for salting fish. There are various accounts of why the village became deserted, one being that all the men were drowned when trying to elude an 18th-century press gang but the answer is probably that, as elsewhere, the shoals disappeared. There are no facilities for food in the village.

Take the road out of Portquin; near the top of the rise the Path leads off to seaward, past a National Trust house.

On Doyden Point is a 19th-century 'folly', Doyden Castle, in which the owner used to stage parties.

By the next stile on the Path is the old shaft of an antimony mine, fenced round.

The Path, good with fine views, continues along the cliffs, all in National Trust territory, bringing you to Lundy Bay, an excellent sandy beach in quiet and green surroundings.

Extract from Letts Guides the first usable guides to the coastal path. Note the inland route from Pine Haven to Port Quin. It is still amazing to reflect how much time, effort and money Cornwall spent in trying to prevent a coastal path here! When they could have had one, for free!

CHAPTER 11

Public Enquiries

Kingswear 1, our first

Let us say at the outset we lost this one in 1976 but it was a pyrrhic victory for the Countryside Commission and Devon County Council. What they technically gained was never even implemented. However that is as Devonians say 'going backsifore'.

The Commission's plan backed by Devon County Council was to use the existing right of way going up behind Mill Bay Cove at Kingswear behind Coleton Fishacre House and back to the coast again at Scabbacombe Head. Needless to say neither the Ramblers' Association nor ourselves thought that this should go through unopposed. In fact the Ramblers considered this case was such an important point of principle that they sent down John Trevelyan, their national assistant secretary, to put their case. We for our part also seeing the significance, decided despite our limited funds to use legal representation. This was Roger Roberts a local solicitor who kindly agreed to act for us at a modest fee.

The enquiry was an uncomfortable one for the Commission and Devon County Council on their inland route. They had expected opposition from us but thought the landowner had acquiesced in their plans because the route was so far inland. However by the time of the enquiry he had changed his mind so that they met resistance from all quarters. There was in fact one most significant moment in the enquiry when the inspector asked for anyone who supported the proposers to show assent. No one spoke up, so he asked a second time again – there was silence. He then remarked that he had to take it that no one but the proposers supported the scheme.

It is lengthy but a local press report next day gives a media view:-

Coastal Walk Plans are a mockery – claim

The Countryside Commission and Devon County Council came under fire at a crowded public enquiry yesterday for allegedly making nonsense of the idea of creating a coast path between Brixham and Kingswear. Representatives of the Ramblers' Association, the South West Way Association and local residents crammed into the Kingswear Hall to voice their objections to one of the most controversial issues in the area in recent years – plans by the County Council to get a public path creation order.

Although they agreed that a coastal path was vital, many objectors said that the proposed scheme made a mockery of the term 'coastal path' because a large proportion of it stretched inland with views of the sea becoming virtually impossible.

Mr R H Roberts, representing the South West Way Association, said that the route from Man Sands to Kelly Cove ceased to be a coast path and ran unnecessarily far inland. 'It would encourage people out of their cars and provide a wonderful walk, but if diverted too far inland it could become just another footpath', he said.

Stumbling

The pathway when complete would be part of the South Devon coast path extending from Lyme Regis to Plymouth and covering 93 miles. The route begins at Man Sands, passes Scabbacombe Sands, and at Scabbacombe Head travels inland to Coleton Fishacre Estate, over agricultural land and finishes at Kelly's Cove.

Mr Peter Holden, for Mr Roland Smith, owner of the Coleton Fishacre Estate, said that both the Countryside Commission and the county council were willing to agree with 'minor deviations' on the northern section of the planned coast path. The main stumbling block was the southern section involving the Coleton estate.

Mr John Trevelyan, assistant secretary of the Ramblers' Association, said that although he supported the plans for a coast path, the inland route proposed in the order made nonsense of the idea of a coast path. They were disappointed that the Countryside Commission was supporting the proposal.

Mr Roberts told the inspector that the South West Way Association thought the County Council was wrong in saying that a public right of way did not exist between Brixham and Kingswear along the cliffs.

The view the authorities did not wish walkers to see, the Mew Stone from Froward Point. The so-called coast path was to be routed inland here. The trees are mostly 100 year old Monterey Pines that suffered heavily in the great gale of 1990 shortly after the picture was taken. The tree is a native of California where a few of it's ancestors escaped an ice age.

Delights

Our association has gone into this very carefully and it seems that the public have been able to enjoy a walk all along the coast from Brixham to Kingswear without any diversions from around the estate.

Old guidebooks refer to the delights of a walk over Berry Head all the way round to Kingswear and there is a right of way map in Torbay Council offices, which was held by, and prepared by Brixham Urban District Council in 1906, showing the coast path as a public right of way all along the cliffs and down to Pudcombe Cove. It is now proposed that the new path, which will involve compensation payments and extra expense, be provided along a much less desirable route.

Wall Pennywort growing above Pudcombe Cove. It grows prolifically on walls and shady hedge banks in some parts of Devon but is scarce in many places elsewhere. The Pennywort is a reference to the leaf's similarity to our old penny when they were 'd' rather than modern 'p'. The alternative name is Navelwort, after the dimple in the middle of the leaf.

Perhaps we overstate the position but as we saw it this enquiry brought home to the Commission that our Association had come to stay and that though they might not like our opinions they were going to hear about them, and publicly, in future. They were still going to try and ride roughshod over potential users' opinions but they were not going to do so unopposed. There were to be other enquiries in the future when we would disagree with them but also some when we were pleased to support. They were certainly never again to engage in 'a war on all fronts': they made absolutely certain in future that at least one side agreed with them.

We said to Devon County's men at the enquiry if they were going to have a fight why not go for something worth having. This suggestion at least seems to have gone home as no other public enquiry in Devon was ever fought except about a truly coastal path.

The inspector did find in favour of the unsatisfactory route on a technicality but as said previously it was never implemented – was the unanimity of opposition the reason? The Countryside Commission gave a grant to the National Trust to buy the Coleton Fishacre Estate. Devon County then came up with a coastal route from Scabbacombe Head, through Pudcombe to Kelly's Cove, which was not opposed in any way. Later there was an opening ceremony near Higher Brownstone Farm.

The final result is the marvellously unspoilt rural stretch of coast path between Kingswear and Brixham; all the more splendid and wonderful bearing in mind its proximity to the largely urban area of Torbay.

Lulworth and Abbotsbury

Both these enquiries were in 1978 and we now fortunately had the services on our Committee of Ron Vinnicombe who was experienced in such matters and therefore led for us. Lulworth was an entire loss for Dorset County Council. A very short section of the spectacular coast path east of Lulworth Cove had become unsafe. Rather than try to move it inland a few yards they suggested a long and unsatisfactory diversion from the road up from Lulworth Cove to West Lulworth. By questioning, it came out at the enquiry that Dorset had not even considered the shorter alternative and that certainly surprised the inspector. We also, at this enquiry, had powerful allies; the Royal Geological Society used this path for field trips and did not want it closed. They sent down learned and very well qualified witnesses to argue that the cliffs were not structurally unsound. There was one telling moment when Dorset County Council put their own geological expert up against the Society's. He was asked what were his qualifications and the Society was quick to ascertain that he only had a lower degree and nothing else!

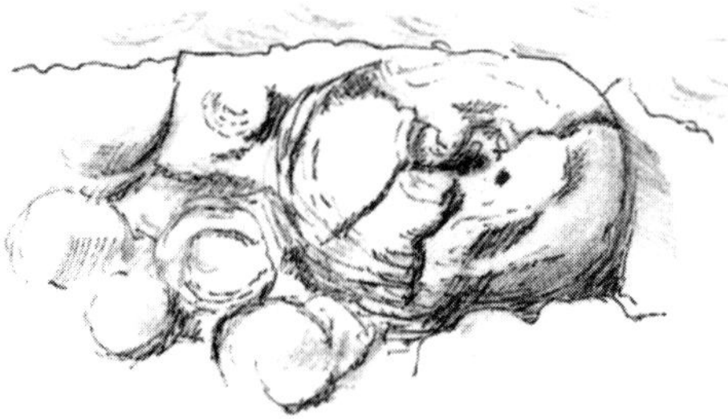

Just inside the western end of the Lulworth Army Range is this fossilized forest. A thought to ponder, it is well over 100 million years old. Not surprisingly it has been declared a Site of Special Scientific interest.

Abbotsbury was an unfortunate win for Dorset County Council backed by the Strangeways Estate. Whether it was intentional or just careless omission on Dorset's part we do not know. However we arrived at the enquiry only thinking we were going to argue over the diversion of a short length of path near New Barn. It turned out it was for a whole stretch of path between Abbotsbury and Langton Herring. We were unprepared for this and our case suffered in consequence. The Strangeways Estate advanced the argument that there could not be a footpath anywhere near the Swannery. This hardly seems a tenable argument when one considers the number of annual visitors to the Swannery

This is a sight that baffles some visitors to Abbotsbury Swannery. They are not hairbrushes on sticks! They are pollarded osier willow trees. The new growth is cut regularly to be made into hurdles or decoys. Decoys are a funnel shaped trap, which were used with the aid of a trained dog to snare wild waterfowl.

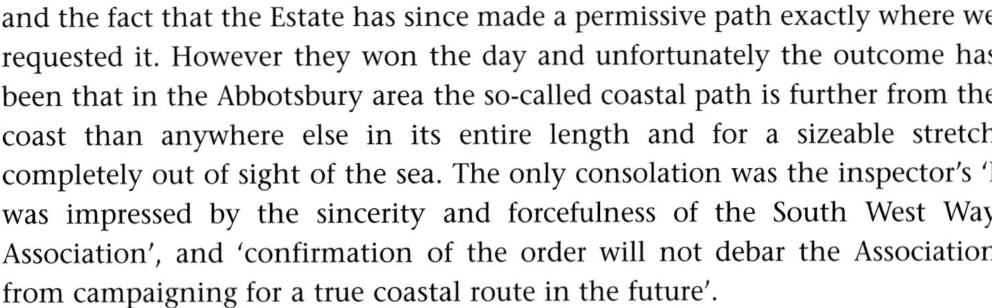

and the fact that the Estate has since made a permissive path exactly where we requested it. However they won the day and unfortunately the outcome has been that in the Abbotsbury area the so-called coastal path is further from the coast than anywhere else in its entire length and for a sizeable stretch completely out of sight of the sea. The only consolation was the inspector's 'I was impressed by the sincerity and forcefulness of the South West Way Association', and 'confirmation of the order will not debar the Association from campaigning for a true coastal route in the future'.

Axmouth

This was an enquiry to try and obtain a more coastal route immediately east of the River Axe. Here the path comes inland and uses an old definitive right of way right through the middle of a golf course. We had hoped for some trade off arrangement thinking the golf course would prefer a route at the side of their property. Unfortunately there were considerable objections to our proposal, principally from Allhallows School, which has since closed.

Widmouth Head

The next enquiry in which we were involved was in 1980 at Ilfracombe into the projected path at Widmouth Head between Combe Martin and Ilfracombe. This was a complete turn round from our previous role. Here we were actively supporting the Countryside Commission at their request and the local authority, to obtain a lovely but in part arduous path from Watermouth around the seaward side of Widmouth Head. We said then:- 'Widmouth Head has superb views, perhaps the most spectacular between Minehead and Hartland Point and that is saying something'. This enquiry was a victory and the lovely path has been fully used ever since, doing away as it did with a long stretch on a busy main road. The chief opposers feared impingement on their private property but there has been no record of any problems to this day.

Widmouth Head from Watermouth: it was here, in the Second World War that trials were effected for the Pipe Line Under the Ocean, Pluto. A public enquiry was fought in 1980 to secure the fine path round Widmouth Head and eliminate a long stretch of road walking.

Kingswear II

This was a public enquiry in 1981 with a difference, all based on submitted written evidence. At the original enquiry Kingswear I, there were objections to the proposed path in front of the old coastguard cottages now summer seasonal lets. The inspector had suggested an alternative route behind the cottages. The Association had in fact decided not to oppose this small section, although they did not like it, hoping that there might be no opposition and that therefore the eastern section as far as Scabbacombe Beach might be opened more quickly. In the event there was opposition and the Association Committee then decided to join the ranks of those who were objecting to the path going behind the cottages.

This time the enquiry, with fresh evidence from local users, found in favour of a path in front of the cottages. The significant thing is that this has never been implemented. Now whilst it can be said this short length is in itself unimportant, the principle is. When we have tried to have a second attempt to improve sections which we have lost at public enquiries e.g. Abbotsbury, we are always firmly told, the inspector ruled against you, that is the end of the matter. Yet here when it suits authority to ignore the inspector's ruling they do so.

Port Isaac

This was an enquiry in 1983 with a difference, but this time it was the line up that was exceptional. The Countryside Commission and our Association were fighting the landowner and Cornwall County Council who opposed a coast path.

The old part of Port Isaac is a most attractive place. Surprisingly a land rover once went through a roof here on 5 November 1999! One of the narrow streets, originally called Temple Bar is called by locals 'Squeeze-ee-belly Alley'.

However to start at the beginning. Ron Vinnicombe and the Secretary 'arranged to go down a little while before to look over the routes, to assist him (Ron), to prepare our case. Unfortunately the day we had chosen proved to be one of unremitting rain. We started from Port Isaac at about 11.00 in the morning walking by the coastal route to Port Quin and then back by the inland route ... We had a packed lunch at Port Quin and it really was raining so hard we looked for somewhere under cover to eat it. We found refuge in a galvanised iron roofed garage and as the rain hammered on the roof could only console ourselves by hoping that if we were successful in getting the coastal route, that conditions would not often be so bad for walkers as they were that day.

'We did wonder if very many Cornish ratepayers, particularly those in the tourist trade, were aware that Cornwall was spending their money to oppose a tourist asset which would have cost Cornwall nothing. The irony of the situation was compounded because Cornwall's case in opposing it was purely on the grounds of cost. Official long distance paths such as the South West Way are 100% grant aided from central government so that it would have cost Cornwall nothing to have the path but here was Cornwall County Council spending money to oppose it.

Before the official Cornish opening ten years ago, there was no problem in walking this particular stretch of coast then. ... The present landowners have made various attempts over the years to prevent usage ... the landowners claim that it would be more difficult fully to farm this particular stretch of coast if there was a coast path. The opposing view was that the whole of the rest of the undeveloped Cornish coast now had a coast path and even with the best will in the world, it was going to be difficult for people to understand that an anomaly existed here. Those opposing the coastal route disagreed that it was an anomaly, but when challenged to name another sizeable area of rural Cornish coast without a coast path, they completely failed to do so.

The outcome was a victory for the coastal route. Cornwall had spent a lot of money opposing the asset they could have had for free. To this day we wonder why? The path even then took a considerable time to complete, not being opened until 1985. As at Pentewan there was an excess of publicly funded unnecessary fencing topped with barbed wire which thankfully was later removed.

This is the Temple of the Wind on Efford Down, Bude, which locals jokingly call the 'Pepper Pot'. It originally was orientated north – south, but became undermined by the sea and was moved inland, when, however, it was re-erected a few degrees out of true.

Bude and Branscombe

Our Secretary attended an enquiry in June 1987 at Bude to try and prevent a housing development on Efford Down that admittedly was not on the coast path but would certainly have marred views from it. There was very considerable opposition to this in the Bude area and it would have affected an access path to the coast path. The result of the enquiry was that the development was stopped. The Secretary also attended an enquiry at Branscombe in September where an attempt was being made to get more path on the coast instead of on a long diversion inland behind a hill completely out of sight of the sea. The result of this enquiry was not quite so successful; we only got 75% of what we had requested. We did however get another small improvement some years later so the final outcome was a much better path.

Lynton

Exmoor National Park, seemingly as ever embarked on their crusade to keep one away from their coast, tried to close the definitive footpath that ran from Countisbury out to Foreland Point near Lynton. They firstly put up notices 'Dangerous Path – Do not use' and then made a closure order. Let us hasten to add that there was no record of an accident on the path and whilst to be fair someone without a head for heights would not have enjoyed it, it was a wide well made path with glorious views.

The inspector, why he allowed himself to be appointed we can not think, conducted the enquiry but then because he did suffer from vertigo refused to walk the path. This did not stop him from trying to rule that the path should be closed when he had never walked it. Needless to say we protested that justice was not being done and won our case. The path remained open and the signs and barriers to prevent access were removed.

Camelford

There were late objections to the re-routing of the path at Buckator on the north Cornish coast. Our Secretary attended the enquiry there and the outcome was as we wished. He did however make this comment:- 'Our route is now "official". We don't suppose this makes much difference to our members who have walked the new route for five years now but it does make one pause as one contemplates the cost of it all. And it was all brought about by three objectors who were not the landowner anyway. He was in complete agreement with the realignment.'

Weymouth Area Roads

Our Chairman represented the Association at two enquires into the A354 Dorchester – Weymouth – Portland road schemes. The first was its link with the A352, and affected the Inland Route. The other was closer to Wyke Regis and would not only affect the coast path but it would also mean altering the designated area of Heritage Coast to accommodate the road. For the first there was a successful outcome with objections being conceded. The second resulted in the road scheme being rejected but with a reservation being made on the land affected.

Weymouth is well remembered as the resort that was made popular by King George III taking to the relatively new idea of sea bathing. It was of course then more of a health promoting dip rather than a swim. Weymouth perhaps is happy not to be so well remembered as being the place where the Black Death came to England!

Charlestown Harbour

An unusual problem occurred in Charlestown, on the south Cornwall coast. A company, called The Square Sail Shipping Company, had purchased the harbour area and wanted to raise funds to repair the harbour walls. They thought that a way to do this would be to charge those going through a toll. Our Association, and indeed many others, were not in favour of paying to use an official Long Distance Path. A public enquiry in 1996 ensued and a right of way without charge was confirmed through the harbour area but not over the lock gates. This had been the usual means of progress when they were closed for many years. In 1997 there was a second enquiry as the result of appeals against the decision that the lock gates were not a right of way. However the same decision was reached; free access through the port area but not across the lock gates. We heard afterwards from Mary Weston of the Ramblers' Association that many local people had been pleased to have our opposition to the closure. This was because:- 'The new owner was under the impression that it was the locals of Charlestown only who were objecting to his plans, and was surprised to discover that other people/organisations were also objectors'.

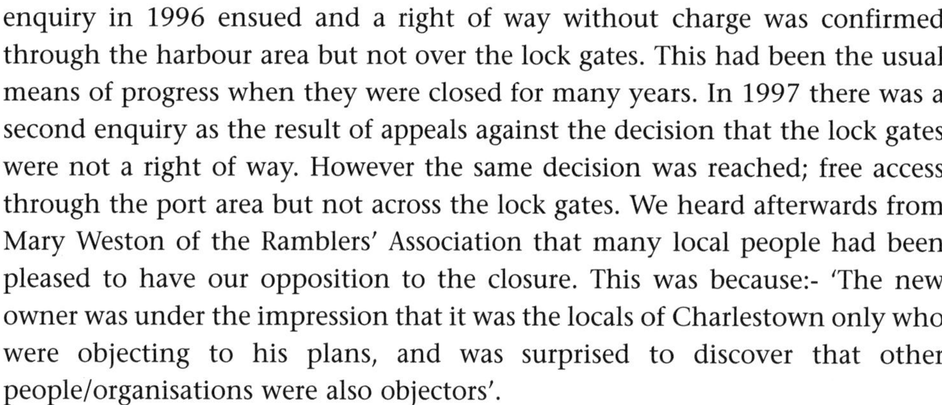

Chapter 12

Newsletters (Later SWCP News)

Our original logo. This was the simple heading we adopted for our early Newsletters from March 1974 onwards.

The first was sent to members in September 1973. Thereafter for a while there were three a year until it was reduced in 1981 to two in an economy drive. The first one to have anything but text was January 1976 when we included a map of the new Lulworth Range Walk because at that stage there was not any map available. The first Newsletters were duplicated on foolscap sheets of paper but later from the autumn of 1979, Newsletter No 10, they became printed A5 size. We had, with acknowledgement, copied the idea from our sister organisation the Offa's Dyke Association.

In the autumn 1979 we printed a piece by Mark Richards on Land's End: 'mingling with the masses can be a traumatic experience, but solitary walkers may delight at witnessing the great British inability to stray more than half-a-mile from the security of the infernal combustion engine and heartily bless this failing. Standing upon Pedn-men-du above Sennen Cove you can let the mind drift seaward unstifled by the presence of pilgrims satisfying their gregarious desire to examine the extremity of our kingdom. The old Cornish name for Dr Syntax's Head, the ultimate in parochialism, was Pedn-an-Laaz, "the end of the World".' The same Newsletter had our first attempt at tabling the tides, it was called 'Tide Tables for Paddlers' and it was drawn up for us by a merchant navy man, Captain Lee of Newton Abbot.

The Capstan House at Sennen Cove was used to pull boats ashore. Perkin Warbeck, who claimed to be one of the princes in the Tower landed at Whitesand Bay and marched on Exeter. Where he came from, may be in doubt, but he certainly ended at the Tower, on the scaffold!

Winter 1979–80 had a piece asking 'why we walk at all'. 'Surely it's not the rain that beats upon one, the wind that cuts through one or the fog and mist which always obscure the best view or even on a more mundane level the seasonal café that shut earlier this year, so denying that hoped-for cup of tea! Could it be the challenge or maybe just the granite walled old daffodil field at Nanjizal, the drifts of white bells above Pentargon waterfall, the sea pinks in their thousands everywhere, the sunset over the sea at Hartland Quay – yes, we will be there – again!' In the spring of 1980 one of our members Laurie Bruce devised a special crossword for us. There were a number of these over the years. Later in the year we had a 'Suggestion for Tough Specimens'. This was to tell them about Sir Leslie Stephen's favourite day walk. He would set out from St Ives to follow the coast around Land's End and back to Penzance then walk across the moors to St Ives. As Tony Collings said no wonder he liked to make an early start, it must have been about 50 miles. Sir Stephen was incidentally a well-known Victorian critic and scholar who was the father of both Vanessa Bell and Virginia Woolf.

In 1982 there was a piece entitled *In a Blizzard for the Special Baby Care Unit* by Eric Wallis. He set out to walk around the Plymouth Hospital catchment area to raise funds for a Cardiac/Respiratory Monitor. His 250-mile route took him westward along the coast to Polperro, northwards to the coast at Boscastle, north-eastwards to Bude, south-east to Okehampton, southwards to Strete and back to Plymouth. The idea was to take in Brown Willy and High Willhays, the highest points in Cornwall and Devon respectively. Although the walk was planned for the end of April 1981 the weather had been against him.

'By the official send-off at the Hospital it was raining. It stayed with me all the way to Looe. ... I splashed through Seaton and as I started to climb out towards the start of the path along the Murrayton/Windsworth section, I beheld in front of me and travelling the same route a Muscovy duck, who looked at me through sheets of rain. ... In the fields above Millendreath huddled in a corner under dripping trees was a little family of Highland cattle. Their long hair hanging straight in wet lines. They looked so forlorn.'

Later Eric stayed overnight at Jamaica Inn. 'A contented evening was spent in front of that fire as the buzz of conversation increased as the Inn filled. ... As the evening wore on so the shriek of wind increased and then great flurries of white stuff burst into the bar every time the door was opened. Eventually a policeman with dark uniform fringed with frost looked in and announced that those who wished to motor east or west had better look slippy because the A30 was beginning to drift over in several places. A mass exodus ensued leaving a few Bolventor regulars and five of us guests.'

In the morning Eric tried to leave but got beaten back by the weather. 'I was in a madhouse, with an odd clump of heather and granite outcrop. It was a slog through a completely white world with millions of snowflakes whizzing away behind me with the speed of bullets. Those that did not whizz away stuck to every seam, entered both sleeves or smashed into cheek and eye like hundreds of little whiplashes. I could not see anything but began to see sense. ...Turn around and retreat southwards. The relief was instant. I could keep my eyes open for a start and I put the compass away. I used the wind for propulsion.'

The next day Eric was able to leave and proceed on his walk taking in Brown Willy. 'The snow was about three inches deep on the exposed places, but huge drifts in the lee of rocks and walls made for tiring leg work. ... There was Brown

Willy revealed in Alpine splendour outlined against the grey sky. ... Clambering up its eastern side was hard work. The drifting on those granite slopes proved dangerous. I frequently disappeared to the waist between hidden granite boulders and at times was climbing on hands and knees.'

After he had finished his walk Eric was invited to see the new piece of equipment in use. 'At that moment I realised that a walk in a blizzard was all worthwhile.'

In autumn 1983 there was a short piece about a tough challenge walk that was held in August every year and had to be completed in twelve hours, 'the Dorset Doddle'. This is basically a walk from Weymouth to Swanage that they describe as thirty-three tough and very scenic miles along the Dorset coast. It has also been recorded that it is not for beginners and those members who have walked this stretch can appreciate that a challenge walk along there is a challenge indeed. Another challenge walk which ran for a number of years was the Mid-Cornwall Coastal Challenge, which was also a 33 mile walk on the South Cornwall coast from St Anthony's Head Lighthouse to Hallane then turning inland to St Austell. On this walk if you completed it on time you got a cup of tea and a Cornish pasty.

St Anthony's Lighthouse marks the eastern entrance to the 'Carrick Roads' Falmouth's extensive natural harbour. The lighthouse was once the starting point for the annual Mid-Cornwall Challenge Walk to cover the 33 miles to St Austell in 12 hours. Those who did so were rewarded with a cup of tea and a pasty.

In autumn of 1984 a Barry Smith wrote to us about some of the literary connections in Cornwall, trivial and profound. 'Swinburne spraining his ankle at Tintagel, a Trollope short story about Bossiney area. Virginia Woolf at St Ives, Dylan Thomas getting married at Penzance!'

1985 had a warning on weever fish which was repeated in 2003. 'The Lesser Weever is only about 15cm (6 inches) long and lies partly buried beneath the surface waiting to catch and eat small shrimps that approach its upwardly directed mouth. However this small, cryptic (concealed) fish must be treated with care for the black dorsal fin has poisonous spines which are raised when it is disturbed and can easily penetrate the unsuspecting swimmer's hand or the paddler's foot. The result is an extremely painful sting that results from the injection of poison into the wound. The sting is a nerve poison and while not fatal, can cause great pain and considerable distress to the victim. ... If someone is unlucky enough to be stung the most effective known treatment is to bathe the wound with very hot water as soon as possible after the sting occurs. The heat breaks down the poison and results in rapid relief from the pain and possible local swelling.'

The Lesser Weever Fish a hazard to those who paddle barefoot. They lie in shallow water under the sand to catch shrimps but have poisonous dorsal fins that can cause severe pain.

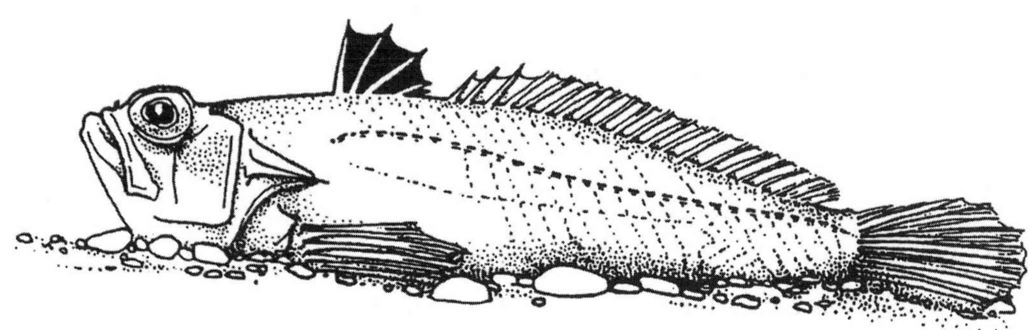

In 1986 we had an item on the Cornish language, part of which is reproduced here.

Hynwyn – Leow Kernewk
(Cornish Place Names)

Many of the place names in Cornwall are of Anglo-Saxon origin of course, particularly in the more easterly parts of Cornwall. A vast number of names, however, come from the Cornish language itself and it is said that in West Penwith, the most Cornish of areas, over ninety percent of the place names derive directly from the Cornish language.

Cornish is one of the Celtic group of languages, whose surviving examples are Irish, Scottish and Manx Gaelic, Welsh and Breton. Cornish is most nearly related to the last of these. Under constant pressure from English, Cornish died out as a spoken language by about 1800, though much of it passed into dialect. During this century, it has undergone a striking revival and is now written and spoken by an increasing band of enthusiasts.

In 1987 Ruth and Don Sanderson, with apologies to John Masefield, sent us a poem 'dedicated to all who walk the path'.

Path-Fever

We must go down to the path again,
To the lovely path and sky,
And all we ask is a safe track and waymarks to guide us by.
And the boots' tramp and the wind's song
And the white clouds flying,
And the ups and downs along the way
And the sea birds crying.

We must go down to the path again,
For the call of the South West Way,
Is a wild call, and a clear call,
That will not go away.
And all we ask is a sunny day
With the white clouds blowing,
And the craggy cliffs and the sea spray,
And the wild flowers growing.

We must go down to the path again,
To the vagrant gypsy life,
To the gull's way, the South West Way,
Where the wind's like a breath of life.
And all we ask is a refreshing bathe,
And drink with a fellow-rover,
And a good meal and a friendly abode,
When the day's trek is over.

In 1988 there was an article by Peter and Joy Dring of Cambridge who had just completed the path. They had walked it in a series of Spring Bank Holidays.

They said:- 'Between us we got sunburnt, drenched, bitten by a dog, chased by a goose, charged by a bullock and even sprayed by slurry! We had aching legs and blistered feet but would not have missed it for the worlds.'

There was also an article by Noel Allen, the Chairman of the Exmoor Natural History Society. 'Selworthy Beacon. There will be the usual woodland birds including the nuthatch, treecreeper, and goldcrest, and joined in April by the summer visiting chiffchaff, willow warbler, and wood warbler from Africa. On the cliffs below only a few pairs of herring gulls nest, though fulmars have been prospecting the cliffs over the past few years, and may soon stay to nest. On the top of North Hill the path emerges on heathland with bell heather and ling, common and western gorse, and wide tracks of bristle grass. The croaking of the raven may well be heard for at least two pairs nest annually on the cliffs here. Whinchats, wheatears, skylarks, and meadow pippits feed and breed among the rocky slopes of the deep combes running down to the sea. Buzzards and kestrels regularly over-fly the heathland peering down in search of rabbits, mice and even beetles, all part of their diet.'

In 1989 we had a number problem:- 'Your Secretary believes that he has at last got it right. The Spring Newsletter should have been 39. Someone said, "he must have been walking the coast path on his head". Another murmured something about his running out of fingers. This is number 40!'

We also had 'A Warning to us All' from Judy Morris who 'had the bright idea for celebrating my 50th birthday – walking the South West Way'. She walked at first with their dog; her husband who had an interest in insects would pursue his hobby and meet her at a prearranged point further along the coast. They would then stay at a B & B and do the same again next day. Starting from Poole they carried this routine out for some years but by the time they reached north Cornwall the dog was too old to walk the distance so stayed in the car with her husband. 'People thought I was very brave to walk on my own but I never had a moment's unease. Everyone I met was very pleasant. I told my husband he would know where to send the search party if I failed to turn up one night as I was on the coast path all the time.

'I arrived at Welcombe Mouth, just in Devon, for our 6.00 pm rendezvous. 6 o'clock came and went and so did 7 o'clock. Had the car broken down? I was cold and penniless. I won't dwell on the next 24 hours – suffice it to say, the police eventually located the car with the dog inside it (alright) and husband half way down a cliff with two broken feet at about 2.00 pm on the next day. The police, rescue services, ambulance and kind B & B lady who took me on trust, were marvellous. All was well in the end – except for the broken feet of course! ... I should have had more money with me ... I should have known more accurately where my husband and car might be. I should have known the number of the car. ... It is not always the obvious candidate who gets into trouble, and be prepared for the unlikely. I was fine!'

It has often been said that the best part of the day's walk is taking ones boots off at the end and, of course, that walker's great delight the cup of tea!

In 1990 Stuart and Louise Shurlock took one of several family holidays with their two daughters Rosemary and Anne walking part of the coast path. They mentioned in their letter a feeling we nearly all have had at sometime. 'The relentless ups and downs made us very grateful for the bed and breakfast at the end, even if it was invariably two miles inland at the top of a steep hill.'

In the same year there was an article 'Golf – An Introduction for Non-Golfing Walkers' by Peter Scott-Malden. We reproduce a paragraph:- 'The golf ball, when hit, starts its flight at over 100 m p h; it may travel 200 yards and is still moving pretty fast when it comes down. If a ball hits you, this is always unpleasant, often painful, and very occasionally fatal. Therefore it makes sense to avoid it.'

In the spring of 1991 there was an article by Dr Alan Castle, secretary of the Long Distance Walkers' Association. He made a point about the strenuous nature of parts of the path. 'But the climbing soon began in earnest as I headed down into Cornwall. The section between Trebarwith Strand and Port Isaac proved to be utterly exhausting. Most of my walking takes place in mountain country and I had mistakenly assumed that the coast path could not possibly be as demanding as hill walking. But I was wrong. I think the problem is that although most of the ascents are relatively short, each one is followed by an equally steep descent, and there are many such ups and downs to a mile. Hence, unlike mountain walking, where a climb can last for several hours, it is difficult to develop any sort of walking rhythm. But the glorious scenery of cliff and sea quickly dispel most feelings of fatigue.'

Wendy Arkel of Halesowen wrote partly on the same theme but put it differently. 'Climbing up the Dodman, which means "Dead Man" was a hard slog on one of the hottest days. By the time I got to the top I felt like a half-Dod-woman! When we reached the pretty village of Gorran Haven we were amused to find a bakery called "Cakebreads", and certainly enjoyed our refreshments there.'

The Dodman was an Iron Age promontory fort that adds to the steepness of the assent. Dodman is a corruption of dead man. The cross was erected in 1896 and is in memory of those who drowned below, this headland when two destroyers HMS Lynx and HMS Thrasher ran ashore.

In 1992 our Secretary reported he had received in the course of the year eight letters from folk who had completed the path. 'All completion letters project pleasure, a sense of achievement and then we sense, a little regret. We congratulate you all even though you do not write to tell us about those memorable days. All is not lost. Come back to the west country again. Put the path under your boots and do it all again – the other way round. We can assure you of another splendid walk and, it is true, it does look different.'

A wild flower enthusiast Andrew Banks from London walked from Starcross to Looe in the first week of May of 1993 and recorded no less than 103 species during that week.

In 1994 there was a completion of a walk around the coast path that had started in 1987 by Stephen Church. A long time you may say but he was a super purist adventurer; he walked every inch, no ferries were used, and every estuary was walked up to the lowest bridge. The estimated mileage of this was 800 miles. 'The variation in scenery encountered as a result made the exercise well worth while, and in many cases riverside paths made for beautiful walking in their own right. Such stretches which spring to mind include the Camel Trail to Padstow, paths round various arms of the Fal, the east side of the Fowey and crossing the Tamar Bridge gave a certain thrill. On the other hand, it also involved some long boring (and occasionally dangerous) road sections, although these are soon forgotten. I don't wish to give the impression that going round the estuaries was the highlight; the wonderful coast path remains that.'

In 1995 there was an article by Paul Hibberd on Berry Head Country Park. 'Ironically it was the quality of the stone itself which caused the demise of a large chunk of the headland – lost to quarrying earlier this century. However there is still plenty of evidence of earlier human activity – the most obvious being Berry Head's two Napoleonic Forts. The main fortifications were built after the outbreak of war with France in 1793. Some twenty-two years later the war was over and the fort was later disbanded, without a single shot having been fired in anger. Both forts are now open for you to explore. ... Berry Head is famous for its guillemots, having been the largest colony on the Channel Coast. ... The North Fort is also home to the Berry Head Lighthouse – reputed to be both the highest and the shortest lighthouse in the country. Confused? – Visit it and I'm sure you will work it out.'

A walking family near Caerhayes Castle, in south Cornwall. Caerhayes was designed by John Nash of Brighton Pavilion and Buckingham Palace fame. Unfortunately the costs ruined the family that commissioned it. Porthluney the nearby beach was used for the filming of part of Hitchcock's Rebecca *and more recently some of the television* Poldark *series.*

Also in 1995 we had a Sentimental Journey; Helen and Robert Hassel had completed the path over a seven-year period. Helen wrote – 'We have walked the entire path in one-week stages over seven almost consecutive years. ... When we started the walk in 1987 I was a last minute replacement for a friend who had dropped out. We had only just started getting to know one another so I was not only wondering whether I would manage the walk, but how well we would get on together! However, we had a lovely time and were soon planning the next year and the next stage. In 1988 we did a second stage and also got engaged. In 1989 we were married but still found time for a week's walking on the path. ... In 1990 I was recovering from major heart surgery, but one of my targets was to be fit enough to do the next section ... which I achieved. ... By 1992 we had reached Seaton with only one more bit to do. However, though I did not know it at the time I was pregnant ... we did not manage to do any of the walk in 1993 ... we had a lovely little boy. In September this year, with grandparents willing to baby-sit, we finally managed the last section.'

The Secretary wrote a postscript to one letter that spoke of over-laden rucksacks:- 'We do warn about carrying too much. This is not the first time Parcel Force has been used to carry gear that has been jettisoned. Your Secretary did it after two days along Offa's Dyke. We suppose the best plan is when you have packed your sack, empty it and then put only half of it back in.' Maybe your author and his wife can add a postscript to a postscript. After some year's experience we now reckon we carry 16-18 lbs each in our packs and that includes camera, maps, waterproofs in fact everything except the day's packed lunch. The only proviso is that it does mean using a laundrette once a week!

A letter from Deborah Cole told of a camping completion in one go, surely some of the comments would bring back memories to others. 'Snow in April, heat-stroke in May, Force 8 gales at any old time, and the usual woeful stories of waterproofs that weren't. But heck what a small price to pay for the absolutely marvellous magical mind-blowing exhilaration of walking the coast path in its entirety. The birds, the wild flowers, THE CLIMBS, the ever-present sound of the sea, THE CLIMBS, the pasties, the country churches, THE CLIMBS, the twinkle in the fisherman's eye, the puttering of his boat, THE CLIMBS, the fox (and cub), the deer, the badger, the weasel, the seal, the buzzards, the kestrel, the slugs, the tick, and THE CLIMBS. God bless them all! ... It is the best thing I have ever done. Oh I almost forgot please can we have our certificate?!'

There were problems about paint on the daymark on the Gribbin near Fowey. The correspondence finished on rather a different subject. 'As a more cheerful footnote, the swans on the lake close to the coast path at nearby Menabilly raised a family of no less than eight cygnets last year. Quite an achievement.'

In 1996 Dorothy Saunders of Taunton completed the path and told of a visit to the Minack Theatre at Porthcurno. 'Everyone else had come by car and we queued in hot sun in light summer clothes. Halfway through the performance clouds gathered, the wind increased, the temperature plummeted and by the end I was clad in anorak, waterproof trousers, mittens and woolly hat while most others shivered, their clothes being in their cars!'

Rowena Cade founded the Minack Theatre in 1935. It is a stunning setting for dramatic performances, the backdrop being the sea. Treryn Dinas in the distance is the site of the one time famous logan (rocking) stone. A Lieutenant Goldsmith, nephew of Oliver toppled it, and though the Admiralty ordered its restoration it has never rocked as it did formerly.

In 1997 reprinted by permission of the *Bournemouth Evening Echo* was an article about the Royal Marines' memorial garden on the coast path high above Chapman's Pool. It bears a message to passing walkers:- 'Rest awhile and reflect that we who are living can enjoy the beauty of the sea and countryside'.

There was news of Brian and Paul Gould of Merriott, a father and son completion. 'Our walk started in 1990 when myself and my nine-year old son started at Minehead and seven wonderful weeks later in 1996, here we are in Poole. ... We started this walk as a father and son but ended it as best mates and a father and young man.' There was also Sandra and Mark Porter, a mother and son completion, Mark began at 10 years old and finished at seventeen. 'Over the years we have become fairly experienced and certainly fitter walkers; then a six-mile walk with a light daypack would have seen me on a stretcher, but over the last three years we have progressed to 15 miles a day with full camping gear in big rucksacks. As well as the fabulous scenery that moved even a super-cool teenager to gasp and say "wow" – in an unguarded moment, there have been times when we both questioned our sanity through a haze of exhaustion. ... I would like to urge all parents with teenagers, or younger, who show the slightest inclination to walk, to get out on the path and tackle it. The uniqueness of the exercise makes for a very special time together when you can really discover one another in a way not possible in the normal run of life.' Ray Green then working at Torbay Hospital ran the path in 26 days raising approximately £1000 for the Exeter and District Kidney Patients' Association.

The newsletter in the spring of 1998 was a special *25 Years Silver Anniversary Edition*. It had a cartoon on its cover, the left half dated 1973, the right half dated 1998, both sides showed a walker setting off along the coast reaching a notice which said 'No Entry Coast Path Not Completed'. If one looked carefully the hirsute walker of 1973 had lost his hair and become bald by 1998! This edition included an item from the *Guardian*:- 'An unnamed act of 1604 protects Cornish residents from trespass actions on cliff tops, as long as they are shouting directions to fishing boats'.

Later in 1998 Andrew Bristow wrote a piece about the monument to the crew of an American Liberator bomber that crashed into Bossington Hill in October 1942. It had been on a mission over the Atlantic aiding RAF Coastal Command and was returning in poor visibility. Sadly only one member of the crew survived; the rest are buried in the American Military Cemetery in Cambridge.

There were also two articles about films that had been partly made on the coast path. A scene from *The Land Girls* that was supposed to represent a beach near Southampton had actually been filmed on the shoreline of Porlock Bay. Those who knew the area well would have been able to pick out Hurlestone Point in the background. The other film was *Amy Foster* and a lot of it was shot at Port Quin. 'The blacksmith's was staged right in the centre of the hamlet just above the sea ... An arch was actually made over the coast path as you left going east to Kellan Head – this served as a doorway to a shop in the film.' The film crew very laudably put up a notice on the 'wrong' side of the door saying the path was still open

There was a letter from Joan Hampton who had taken 12 years to complete:- 'I feel very privileged to have been given the health and strength to enjoy walking this wonderful route – it has been one of the greatest joys of my retirement. Many happy memories of my walk spring to mind – the folk I have met, short friendly chats with fellow walkers and local people, helpful B & B hosts. The flowers – the banks of thrift in varying shades of pink, paths bordered with bluebells and red campion, patches of yellow kidney vetch, primroses peeping out from rocks, tiny blue squills, the occasional orchid and many more. The birds – gulls wheeling and diving, tiny brown birds who sing from tops of bushes and fly off – apparently laughing – before one can identify them, and sometimes the sight of a raven or peregrine falcon. All these combined with the sheer beauty of cliffs; sky and sea make the walk an unforgettable experience.'

Pale blue Spring Squills are always associated with the Cornish Coasts and it is certain they are prolific in places there. They do however grow elsewhere.

Victoria Taylor who completed the path with her friend Ruth Saxby in 1999 said simply 'I consider this walk to be one of the most wonderful things I have ever done in the whole of my life'. In the same year there was a completion by Alexander Jones that has to be a record – he was 8½ months old and pity his dad he weighed 20lbs! Shirley Alborough who completed the path with her husband Dennis had a somewhat different inspiration to walk the path. 'Many years ago I lived in Bude in North Cornwall and would see the acorn signs when out and about with my two young daughters, and I used to joke to them that one day I'm going to see where they lead to.' She continued 'Well, now I know!'. Our secretary was asked in a letter from Holland for 'the time schedule of fairies'!

Steve Aikenhead of Vermont USA sent this poem.

Lost

Hello. I'm lost. Could you tell me the way?
To Pepper Hole, Butter Hole, or Booby Bay?
They're close to the place I'm supposed to have been

By three. Penallick? Penhallic? It begins with a Pen.
Near Diggory Island? I think it's just north
Of Porth Mear, Porthcothan, or Mawgan Porth.
I know at Porth-Cadjack, Porthgwidden, Hell's Mouth
Towanroath. Or Porthtowan I'd be too far south.
Not Pentire or Pengirt, but still past the Zawn.
It sounds like some place to which I have gone
Back at Dizzard and Pigsback, Squelch Rocks and the Strangles.
Pencanno? Oh, dear – it's jingles and jangles.
Wait! Silly me. It's not Pen. Just listen
To this – it's Porth! Porthmissen!

This is the Towan Roath shaft of the Wheal Coates mine. It was used as the frontispiece of Daphne du Maurier's Vanishing Cornwall. Wheal means mine in Cornish.

Although a great number of walkers finish the path at either South Haven Point or Minehead there are others who walk it in less a continuous fashion and finish it in all sorts of places along the way. The writer was, for instance, once invited to share a celebratory cake at Hartland Quay. However one couple, a Mr and Mrs Line of Goring by Sea, finished in style at the Burgh Island Hotel at Bigbury. They had sent on a suitcase in advance so although they arrived in walking kit with rucksacks they could change and go down to dinner. The lady however had forgotten to pack shoes so was wearing her evening gown with walking boots!

In the autumn of 2000 there were two rather different posts scripts. Mark Baker wrote:- 'Your guide book is a tremendously useful tool, very well thought out, almost a substitute for thought'. Ann Richards had a problem obtaining information on her computer:- 'Has anyone called up the South West Coast Path website and got the Saffron Walden Communist Party? What a difference an org.uk rather than a co.uk makes!!'

Newsletters of 2001 had plenty to offer. An early piece of advice on using buses from Carl Litsinger of Virginia, USA bears repetition. 'A word of warning to the uninitiated; the bus timetables are Byzantine. However, with careful study most folks can sort them out and will discover that almost any section of the coast path can be accessed by bus. Our biggest frustrations were the reduced weekend schedules and poor off season service. In the end, after the fine print was scrutinised and every footnote deciphered, the schedule gave the needed information, and I could plan accordingly. Here's a final hint to bus schedule users; try to settle into a pleasant place on Saturday evening because you're unlikely to go anywhere on Sunday!'

Ruth Jones had never intended to walk the coast path – but did! She moved to Devon and started by accident! She was lured by a beautiful stretch of coastline to walk 'walk about two miles – and then, having fortified myself with a cream tea, huff and puff my way back again. (I wasn't used to hills). ... It became easier to leave the car behind so I didn't have to double back. Gradually it dawned on me that I was not just walking along the coast but walking THE coast path. Moreover I was enjoying myself immensely. Suddenly, I had become a walker.' It took her six years and she said her most memorable moments were sunset at Hartland Quay and the magical scenery around the Helford Estuary.

Steve White had an incident on the path that surely does not befall many. 'Black Head, I was walking alone – it was winter and very quiet, and suddenly I heard a rustling sound behind me. I turned and a man on the end of a parachute landed behind me! It gave me quite a start. The man told me he was paragliding and ran out of thermals, which necessitated an emergency landing. He figures that if he landed near me I would have been able to help him if he had sustained an injury.'

Matthew Cozens caused our Secretary astonishment by his query. 'I have just had the privilege of being able to walk the length of the South West Coast Path in its entirety. It was one of the most rewarding and challenging events to have occurred in my life. It served to make me realise just what a beautiful corner of the world the South West of England really is. Ever since completing the walk I've yearned to retrace my steps and relive the whole experience. I very much hope to, one day, be able to undertake that journey again. With what I have in mind I was wondering if you might be able to answer a question of mine. Do you know it anyone has ever walked the length of the coast path from Minehead to Poole, and then, without pausing walked back to Minehead to make a complete journey of some 1200 miles?' The answer was simply 'NO' so there is still a challenge out there for those who like to be first!

Mary and Calvin Batchelder of New Hampshire made this point. 'It was very satisfying to see the old towns that have given their names to many newer ones in our part of the USA – Plymouth, Falmouth, Bideford, Dartmouth and Weymouth come to mind. However, the warmest memory is of the friendliness of the people we met along the way.'

An article appeared on the interesting ruin at Elberry Cove between Brixham and Paignton. It was a rare sea-bathing house. The lower floor had both a cool plunge and a heated salt-water pool. On a higher floor was a kind of furnished summerhouse for taking meals and entertaining guests. It was part of the Churston Estate, first recorded in the 1840s and last used in the 1920s. There was a jetty alongside and King Edward VII, whilst Price of Wales, landed there in 1879. It is known that servants were sent down in the mornings to light the boiler to heat the water. Lydia, the present Duchess of Bedford had used it as a girl and wrote 'it was the loveliest little dream place' accessed by a 'very prickly path down through the woods'. Next time when you pass by this sad ruin, spare a thought for it, as it once was a centre of leisured living.

This is the one time bathing house of Lord Churston at Elberry Cove near Paignton. It contained both a cold plunge and a heated seawater pool with a reception room above, for eating, or entertaining. A reminder here, if it should be needed, that names can vary. Although the Ordnance Survey use Elberry, more commonly locally it is Elbury and it has also been Helbury and even Elbinny!

Winifred Mary Rodber, who is known to many as Mollie of Minehead, completed the path in stages, camping, at the age of 75. We are not sure but we think 25 years to complete is probably the longest yet. At the risk of repeating ourselves we are certain it's the pasties and cream teas that keep us old ones going.

Marion and Peter Maher from the Wirral made points that others have made:- 'we also found that "strenuous" does mean "STRENUOUS". The walk has been part of our lives for so many years and we are not quite sure how to follow on from here.'

An American walker Peter Seed of Minnesota was warned a gale was coming with this piece of old folklore: 'Mackerel skies and mares' tails make tall ships carry small sails'.

Some people, David White-Jones and his wife, for example like the Taw/Torridge estuary section. 'We are older walkers. We take it all slowly, and enjoy what each section has to offer. The Braunton Burrows are unique, and along the Taw Estuary we were lucky enough to be walking at low tide. There were waders galore, including curlews, oyster-catchers of various descriptions, egrets etc. The view along the Taw Estuary at low tide is quite beautiful, and we urge everyone not to force-march through this section with their eyes closed! At our age two easy sections come as a bit of a break and fortify us for the tough sections to come from Westward Ho!'

There are reputedly 21 Gull Rocks or Mewstones, to use their old name off the coast path. In the autumn of 2002 was a competitive entry listing 20 but with one space left blank because we could not name it. We invited readers to fill the gap, but we are still waiting, so maybe it was only 20 after all. Staying with birds, the feathered variety, choughs were also mentioned. There has been a welcome, if engineered, return of this attractive species. Not only are they the emblematic bird of Cornwall but anyone who has seen their incredible tumbling flight will be glad to see them back in the county again. In the same edition was an item on Walking in Cornwall in 1902. Patrick Doyle of Ontario, Canada had sent our Secretary a copy of his grandfather's diary that he had kept on a walking tour in that county. He started from Cardiff by getting the steamer to Ilfracombe and the train from there to Devonport, an itinerary that would not be possible today. His breakfast at Falmouth might also seem unlikely now 'plaice – with Cornish cream etc'.

Gull Rock off Trebarwith. There are at least twenty gull rocks or mew stones, along the coast path. Mew is the old name for seagull.

End of path markers were at a stage of one there and one to go, so there was still disappointment for those finishing at South Haven Point. Margaret and David Worthington put it this way. 'It was a glorious afternoon as we strode purposefully along the Studland Beach towards South Haven Point, eyes searching eagerly for the familiar tunics of a Royal Marine Band to play us in – banners, streamers, a balloon or two? Nothing! No marker, no focal point to put the seal on those fourteen years of hard endeavour. So the occasion fell flat and it has taken us a few days to lift our spirits as we realise something major has gone out of our lives.'

Kathryn and John Hindson took 5 years and wrote of the rhythm of the path. 'We have too many happy memories of the path to list them all, but the most memorable highlights to us include: Cornish fishing villages, spring flowers, wading the Erme (on a beautifully sunny day), the field boundaries, ... the beer, and of course the wonderful scenery. Perhaps the best of all is the "rhythm of the path" as we called it. Up for breakfast, walk straight out onto the path, and nothing to worry about except where to choose to spend the night (accommodation in May/June not usually being a problem). Good to be so stress-free, and with our usual 100 miles in 8-10 days we could really wind down.'

This year, 2002, saw a family achieve a completion – they were Diana, and Peter Radford and their three children Lucy 10, Daniel 8 and Anna 5, when they started, but a good deal older when they finished six years later! They started rather naturally with a low mileage every day 'they enjoyed every inch of the way with us, paddling or swimming on almost every walk regardless of season. We wanted a way of introducing them to the great outdoors and its wildlife, without the dangers associated with mountain walking, and for this the South West Coast Path takes some beating. Escape routes are plentiful and easy refreshments (and ice creams) are never far away, beach stops can be planned in and it's easy to ensure that no route is too long and arduous. The path winds through some of the best coastal scenery in Europe and for public access it must be one of the best coastlines in the world.'

Another family from Chilcompton near Bath, paralleled the Radford's achievement. These were the Brittons, Alison and Stephen with their three children, Matthew, Nicholas and Sarah. Sarah did not start as young as Anna Radford at five but waited to a mature age of eight, before starting walking. However both girls accomplished the splendid feat of completing the path by the time they were eleven!

'An experience we will remember long after we have hung up our boots for the last time', said John Page.

Margaret Parkes wrote:- 'My son and I have just completed the path after a struggle for me around Lulworth Ranges and Kimmeridge as I am now 70. We have walked the path in seven sections as per the book but we did the first section in 1989 and we were not able to do any more until 1996 since when we have done a section each year. We have enjoyed every minute of it even in pouring rain. We have had some wonderful overnight stays and met some lovely people. I would recommend this walk to anybody.'

The Longships Lighthouse off Land's End, Enys Dodman and the Armed Knight are nearby rocks. Vernon Ward painted a well-known picture of them.

A sculptor, Tom Millard, of Kings Heath walked the path over six years in a somewhat unusual fashion, but fair enough he did it! 'In the context of the sculpture I wanted the journey to be predominately towards the Atlantic, so having started at Minehead and rounded Land's End and the Lizard, I started again at Poole and finished the walk at the Helford River.' He added:- 'Finally, two maxims; there is no such thing as "waterproof" and always walk towards a hot shower or your own car!'

A great number of people have walked the whole or part of the path as a sponsored event for charity, far too many to name them all. However just to give a flavour of what some have done, four at random from 2002. Richard Venables of Hampton raised money for the Shooting Star Trust to build a children's hospice in south west London. Jennifer Rowlandson of Stoodleigh, Devon, walked to fund the repair of St Margaret's Church in her home parish. Mavis Jarvis of Bulmer, York was collecting for Macmillan Cancer Research and Jill Follett of Harbourne, Birmingham supported the RNLI.

John Henton of Billericay asks:- 'Why is there a stile at the top of every steep hill?'

Alison Garthwaite of Leeds wrote this in 2003. 'It surprises me how few of your correspondents mention the delights of the west country towns through which we walkers pass. Among my favourite coast path memories are two nights of local celebration in Westward Ho! and Ilfracombe, both of which I came upon unexpectedly after a long day's walking. In Westward Ho! in August 2000 the town enjoyed a week-long music festival. As I walked along the pebbly beach I heard country and western songs from a folk duo, playing in the open, while line dancers and ballroom pairs measured their steps on the greensward. I sat under the stars, drinking beer and soaking up the atmosphere. There was also a photo exhibition of North Devon life, put on at the Beaford Community Arts. A magical evening.

'In Ilfracombe – a town I love, for its friendly youth hostel, tunnel beaches, tors (hills) and night fishing from the harbour – I arrived in 2002 after 17 miles into the start of the carnival procession. Most of the town seemed to be either on the floats or crowding the pavements and hillsides, waving and laughing. I drank shandy and ate fish and chips as Uncle Tom Cobley And All (an actual float with wooden horse and songs by the Wurzels) his many companions passed very very slowly by. Another brilliant and free evening's entertainment.'

The Finest Walk in the World

This description had been applied to a number of walks, The Milford Track in New Zealand, the Overland Track (Cradle Mountain Trail) in Tasmania, the Tour of Mont Blanc in France, Italy and Switzerland and finally our very own South West Coast Path (South West Way). What in fact makes a walk a fine one? Is it just the exercise and the 'feel good' factor that follows? Is it that there is often the element of fresh fields and pastures new? How high do we rate the scenery and the fact we very often know we are visiting places we could not have seen unless we had come on foot? For some it is the incidental interest of historical, literary or other interests. Many walk to see the local flora and fauna. All these things can make up the total experience; and let us admit, the company, the weather and other hazards can make or mar even the most potentially first class walk.

The article then went on to discuss the other paths but finished with our own. Civilisation certainly but surprisingly long stretches where it seems very far away. More facets of interest than any of the other paths. The sea with all its kaleidoscopic changing moods is a constant companion. You will have to forego the mountain tops but otherwise there is a tremendous variety of scenery and flora and fauna. Perhaps to many of us, it is a lot easier and less expensive to reach!

Right: *View of the Mitre at Milford Sound, South Island New Zealand, this spectacular mountain rises straight from the sea at the end of the Milford Track*

Below: *Cradle Mountain from the Overland Track in Tasmania, it is summer in Australia, so note the snow!*

Chapter 13
Conclusion

This picture shows you what a long distance path can do to a walker. In fact the picture is cheating, it is taken at Kirk Yetholm and the walker has only walked the Pennine Way, less than half the distance of our path!

So that is the story of a path and of an idea, born out of frustration, some thirty years ago. A fair question though, what has been achieved? The fact that the Association spawned by that original idea is still going could be taken to mean that nothing has been accomplished. Alternatively it could be said, especially as the membership is greater than it has ever been, that the case for its activities have been proven.

In truth it is very difficult to know just how much impact an organisation such as ours has actually had. Undoubtedly the authorities' initial ideas for a coast path were extremely poor. Literally miles and miles of it were not on the coast and it was not even to be continuous; there were a whole series of gaps where no path was intended. Even now not everything is perfect, but certainly the path is better routed and maintained than it has ever been.

There are though still problems where too much favour is shown to landowners and not enough consideration to walkers. Authorities such as the Exmoor National Park steadfastly refuse to improve the walking experience. However the set up to manage the path overall is better now, and there is at least a willingness to listen, even if our ideas are not always acted on. However, sometimes, we wonder is too much time spent on reorganisation schemes and 'empire building' rather than more useful administration?

Not every idea that comes to one when 'lost and brambled, hot and sticky' endures for thirty years and attracts some thousands of others to join the crusade. These days when our Association has a website, owns computers, fax and answering machines, it seem very far away from those early days when we did not even possess a typewriter! However, what has been achieved has largely been thanks to those working enthusiastically 'to put something back'. So the last word must go again to all named and unnamed who have so freely given of their time.

Bibliography

BOOKS
Cherry, Bridget and Pevsner, Nikolaus, *The Buildings of England Devon* (1997)
Collings, A G, *Along the South West Way* Part 1 Minehead to Bude (1986)
Cornish Federation of Women's Institutes *The Cornwall Village Book* (1991)
Dawson, Peter, *The South West Way* (1983)
Devon Federation of Women's Institutes *The Devon Village Book* (1990)
Hoskins W G *Devon* (1954)
Newman, John, and Pevsner, Nikolaus, *The Buildings of England Dorset* (1999)
Pevsner, Nikolaus, *The Buildings of England Cornwall* (1996)
Pyatt, Edward, C *Coastal Paths of the South West* (1971)
Richards, Mark, *Walking the North Cornwall Coastal Footpath* (1974)
Smith, Graham, *Something to Declare, lOOO years of Customs and Excise* (1980)
South West Coast Path Association *A History* (1998)
The Coastguard Agency *The History of HM Coastguard* (1995)
Wallington, Mark *500 Mile Walkies* (1986)
Webb, William, *Coastguard! An Official History of HM Coastguard* (1976)
Records of HMCoastguard, Records Information No 8, PRO

GUIDES
Letts Guide
Ward, Ken, and Mason, John, HN *The South-west Peninsula Coastal Path*
1 Minehead to St Ives, 2 St Ives to Plymouth, 3 Plymouth to Poole. (1977)

NATIONAL TRAIL GUIDES
These started as HMSO Guides the original four being:
Somerset and North Devon Coast Path by Gunnel, Clive (1981)
Cornwall Coast Path by Pyatt, Edward, C. (1976)
South Devon Coast Path by Le Messurier, Brian, (1980)
Dorset Coast Path by Jackman, Brian, (1979)
They have since improved their format and there have been several changes of author. They are presently all called *South West Coast Path* and the four titles are: Minehead to Padstow, Padstow to Falmouth, Falmouth to Exmouth and Exmouth to Poole.

SOUTH WEST COAST PATH ASSOCIATION
Annual Guide, The Complete Guide to the Longest National Trail.
Reverse Guide re-issued periodically, Poole Harbour (South Haven Point) to Minehead.

Path Descriptions the Association produces over 50 of these that cover the whole path and are up-to-date detailed descriptions of short sections; these are listed below:

Minehead to Porlock Weir (9.5 miles/15.3 km)
Porlock Weir to Lynmouth (12.3 miles/19.8 km)
Lynmouth to llfracombe (18 miles/30 km)
llfracombe to Croyde Bay (13.6 miles/21.9 km)
Croyde Bay to Barnstaple (16 miles/25 km)
Barnstaple to Westward Ho! (19.1 miles/30.7 km)
Westward Ho! to Clovelly (11.2 miles/18 km)
Clovelly to Hartland Quay (10.3 miles/16.6 km)
Hartland Quay to Bude (15.4 miles/24.8 km)
Bude to Crackington Haven (10.2 miles/16.4 km)
Crackington Haven to Tintagel (12 miles/20 km)
Tintagel to Port Isaac (8 miles/13 km)
Port Isaac to Padstow (11.7 miles/18.9 km)
Padstow to Porthcothan (13.6 miles/21.8 km)
Porthcothan to Newquay (11.1 miles/17.9 km)
Newquay to Perranporth (11 miles/18 km)
Perranporth to Portreath (12.2 miles/19.7km)
Portreath to Hayle (12.4 miles/19.9 km)
Hayle to Pendeen Watch (19.5 miles/31.3 km)
Pendeen Watch to Porthcurno (15.6 miles/25.2 km)
Porthcurno to Penzance (11.5 miles/18.5 km)
Penzance to Porthleven (14 miles/22.5 km)
Porthleven to The Lizard (13.9 miles/22.3 km)
The Lizard to Coverack (10.6 miles/17.1 km)
Coverack to Helford (13.1 miles/21.1 km)
Helford to Falmouth (10 miles/16.1 km)
Falmouth to Portloe (13.7 miles/22 km)
Portloe to Mevagissey (12.3 miles/19.8 km)
Mevagissey to Charlestown (7.2 miles/11.6 km)
Charlestown to Fowey (10.3 miles/16.6 km)
Fowey to Polperro (7.1 miles/11.5 km)
Polperro to Looe (5.0 miles/8.0 km)
Looe to Portwrinkie (7.6 miles/12.2 km)
Portwrinkle to Plymouth (13.3 miles/21.4 km)
Plymouth (River Tamar) to Wembury (River Yealm) (14.8 miles/23.8 km)
Wembury (Warren Point) to Bigbury-on-Sea (13.5 miles/21.8 km)
Bigbury to Salcombe (13 miles/21 km)
Salcombe to Torcross (12.9 miles/20.8 km)
Torcross to Dartmouth (10 miles/16 km)
Dartmouth to Brixham (10.8 miles/17.3 km)
Brixham to Shaldon (19 miles/30 km)
Shaldon to Exmouth (7.9 miles/12.7 km)
Exmouth to Sidmouth (13.1 miles/21 km)
Sidmouth to Lyme Regis (17 miles/27 km)
Lyme Regis to West Bay (9.7 miles/15.6 km)
West Bay to Abbotsbury (9.4 miles/15.2 km)
Abbotsbury to Weymouth (14 miles/23 km)
Isle of Portland (14 miles/22 km)
Weymouth to Lulworth Cove (11 miles/18 km)
Lulworth to Kimmeridge, Lulworth Range (7 miles/11 km)
Kimmeridge to South Haven Point, Poole Harbour (20 miles/31 km)
Alternative Inland Route, West Bexington to Osmington Mills (18 miles/28 km)

Introduction to the Map

SHOWING SOUTH WEST COAST PATH IMPROVEMENTS

(see Map pages 156–157)

Over the years approximately a fifth of the coast path has been improved. This is shown on the following pages with a sketch map of the South West peninsula showing some 93 numbered locations that are then identified by name with a brief description of the improvement (or in some cases comment).

The scale of the map does not allow us to show the many minor, yet important improvements. All of the improvements provide for an improved route closer to the coast, or involve moving the route off roads. We like to think that our Association has been instrumental in achieving many of these improvements by continual pressure on the authorities. However this is not the end of the story as there still are many sections, some major and many minor that are in need of improved realignment. These are now recognised and recorded by the SWCP Team and the managing authorities. Moreover with its increasing membership and improving financial situation the Association now has a fund that is available to make contributions to the cost of suitable path improvements.

In all of this it has been the aim of the Association to increase the enjoyment and the coastal experience of the path users of this wonderful coast path.

In the descriptions that follow there will be reference to the 'official' route. The reason for this is the enabling legislation (National Parks and Access to the Countryside Act 1949) to designate long distance paths (now called National Trails) requires that the relevant government minister has to approve of the route (or changes to it). You will also find that the original route often started and stopped at the edge of towns and some of the larger villages without a proper route between those points. This often caused problems for users, particularly finding the way out of such settlements on to the coast path again. This too has been addressed by the authorities.

SOMERSET & EXMOOR NATIONAL PARK

1 MINEHEAD
A coastal route on existing rights of way and public land from the town via Greenaleigh Farm and up Burgundy Chapel Combe is available and would make a better coast path.

2 THE RUGGED COAST PATH
Over 3 miles long, this superb permissive path from North Hill to the top of Hurlstone Combe gives a true coastal experience denied by the inland official route and the stubbornness of the Exmoor National Park Authority and the National Trust to make it the official route.

3 PORLOCK WEIR
Coast path originally routed behind hotel – now routed on right of way in front of hotel.

4 CULBONE CHURCH TO YENWORTHY
The current route is inland although the earlier 2.5-mile coastal route over which there were safety fears still exists and could be reinstated.

5 GLENTHORNE
Coastal route provided from Wheatham Combe to Wingate Combe. A permissive route close to Glenthorne that existed at one time is no longer used.

NORTH DEVON

6 COUNTISBURY HILL
Coastal route provided north of most of A39 road. Originally a section of the coast path was routed south of this road.

7 VALLEY OF ROCKS
Original route on a section of road east of Lee Abbey, the coast path is now provided on a parallel path.

8 CROCK POINT
Coast path removed from road and around Crock Point.

9 WOODY BAY TO HEDDON VALLEY
The original coast path was routed on an old coach road above and further from the sea even though a

lower and better route existed on public rights of way. The official route is now provided closer to the coast.

10 TRENTISHOE
The original route of the coast path went up from Hunter's Inn passing Trentishoe church. Now there is a more coastal route from Heddon Valley to East Cleave.

11 TRENTISHOE COMMON
Path has been taken off a section of road and provided closer to the coast.

12 WIDMOUTH HEAD
Path now provided on coast. At an early stage much of the route between Combe Martin and Ilfracombe was on the main road until a public enquiry secured a better route.

13 ILFRACOMBE
Originally a coast path route was not in place through the town. An official route is now provided.

14 SAUNTON TO BRAUNTON
The original coast path went on a more direct route via inland country lanes and footpaths. Now it is routed via Braunton Burrows, Crow Point and Hornsey Island to Velator.

15 VELATOR (BRAUNTON) TO BARNSTAPLE (NORTH)
Originally there was not a coast path on this 5-mile section. Now provided.

16 BARNSTAPLE
Originally a coast path route was not provided through the town. An official route is now provided.

17 STICKLEPATH (BARNSTAPLE SOUTH) TO INSTOW
Originally there was no coast path on this 6-mile section. Now provided.

18 INSTOW TO BIDEFORD
Originally there was no coast path on this 3-mile section. Now provided.

19 BIDEFORD TO APPLEDORE
Originally there was no coast path on this 3-mile section. Now provided.

20 APPLEDORE TO WESTWARD HO!
Originally there was no coast path on this 4-mile section. Now provided.
As shown by 15–20 above a coast path was not scheduled for the 21 miles from Braunton to Westward Ho!

21 GREEN CLIFF TO WORTHYGATE WOOD
A series of minor improvements has been made closer to the coast.

22 HIGH WORTHYGATE (GAUTER'S POOL) TO BUCK'S MILLS
More coastal route provided thanks to a National Trust initiative.

23 FORMER BIDEFORD BAY HOLIDAY PARK
More coastal route provided.

24 WINDBURY POINT
The path was scheduled to pass in the valley behind the point. The sabotaged bridge here provided the defining moment in the conception of our Association.

25 STANBURY ACRE POINT TO EAST TITCHBERRY CLIFF
More coastal route provided from Chapman's Rock along Fatacott Cliff, Gawlish Cliff and via Eldern Point. The original idea was to use an inland bridleway.

26 BARLEY BAY
More coastal route provided. This was one of the first serious improvements to provide a seaward path when the fence around the radar station was moved back.

27 HARTLAND QUAY
Original path was routed directly from The Rocket House to north of Screda Point. Coastal route now provided via the quay.

28 SANDHOLE CLIFF
More coastal route provided near Nabor Point.

CORNWALL

29 WIDEMOUTH SANDS (NORTH)
More coastal route provided.

30 MILLOOK
Coast path taken off road onto coastal route via Bridwill Point.

31 BYNORTH CLIFF
More coastal route provided.

32 CLEAVE STRAND
More coastal route provided in place of longer inland detour through a farmyard.

33 BUCKATOR
More coastal route provided.

34 FIRE BEACON POINT
A more coastal route provided from this point to the approach to Pentargon.

35 DUNDERHOLE POINT
More coastal route provided.

36 DENNIS POINT
More coastal route provided.

37 PORT ISAAC TO PORT QUIN
Completely new section of 3 miles of coast path provided in place of inland route. This was secured at a public inquiry despite Cornwall County Council's strenuous objection to a truly coastal path.

38 PORT QUIN
Coastal route provided near Doyden Point.

39 HOLYWELL
Coastal route provided avoiding Holywell village and then via Penhale Point and Ligger Point to Penhale Sands. The path was originally on a long

inland loop via Ellenglaze and Mount to circumvent a military area.

40 PORTREATH
More coastal route provided around Western Hill and on North Cliffs avoiding a road section.

41 GWITHIAN SANDS
Provision of new bridge over Red River provides for coastal route avoiding nearly half a mile of the busy narrow Churchtown Road.

42 HAYLE TOWANS TO LELANT TOWANS
Originally a coast path route was not provided on this 2.5-mile section. Although unavoidably largely on roads an official route is now provided and even this route has been improved from the original.

43 PORDENACK POINT
Path provided closer to the coast.

44 PERCELLA POINT
Path re-routed on to more coastal rights of way.

45 MOUSEHOLE TO NEWLYN
Originally there was no coast path on this 2-mile section. Coast path official route formerly on road now re-routed onto cycleway.

46 NEWLYN TO PENZANCE
Originally a coast path route was not provided on this 2-mile section. An official route is now provided although it is often on the road.

47 PENZANCE STATION TO HELIPORT
Coast path now off-road and provided along sea wall between railway and beach.

48 VELLAN HEAD
Coast path re-routed on to coastal right of way.

49 BLACK HEAD, SOUTH OF COVERACK, TO CHYNALLS POINT
A more coastal route was provided in two stages. Black Head to Chynalls Cliffs was accomplished some years ago but the notorious inland deviation by the piggery to circumvent the one time Headland Hotel took many years of pressure to accomplish.

50 MAENPORTH TO NEWPORTH HEAD
More coastal route provided.

51 FALMOUTH
More coastal and off road route has now been provided on the east side of Pendennis Head.

52 BROOM PARC
New zigzag path provided to do away with incredibly long and steep wooden steps.

53 PORTHLUNEY COVE (EAST)
More coastal route provided.

54 GREEB POINT TO WEST OF HEMMICK BEACH
More coastal route provided.

55 DODMAN POINT TO CADYTHEW ROCK
More coastal route provided.

56 PENTEWAN TO PHOEBE'S POINT
Originally an inland road route. Coastal route now provided.

57 BLACK HEAD, NEAR HALLANE
More coastal route provided after National Trust purchased an old rifle range, in part aided by a donation from our Association.

58 GRIBBIN HEAD
Coastal route provided around headland.

59 PENCARROW HEAD
Coastal route provided around headland.

60 BODIGGA CLIFF TO SEATON
Coast path originally all on roads – now most of the route is a true coast path.

61 DOWNDERRY TO PORTWRINKLE
Coast path originally mostly on roads. A fine coastal route now provided from Battern Cliff eastwards.

62 TREGANTLE RANGES
New permissive coast path takes route off busy roads when range is not in use.

63 TREGANTLE DOWN TO WIGGLE CLIFF
New undulating coast path provided to take almost all of this route via Freathy off-road.

64 MOUNT EDGCUMBE PARK.
Coastal route provided from Redding Point to Raven's Cliff.

SOUTH DEVON

65 CITY OF PLYMOUTH
Originally a coast path route was not provided through the city from the Cremyll ferry to Turnchapel. An official route is now provided from Stonehouse by a 7-mile city waterfront route. Later additions have been a path around Mount Batten Point and the coast path taken off-road beyond Jennycliff.

66 MOTHECOMBE TO RIVER ERME
Coastal route now provided from Battisborough Cove avoiding long inland detour mainly on roads.

67 CHALLABOROUGH TO BIGBURY-ON-SEA
More coastal route provided to take path off-road.

68 BIGBURY-ON-SEA
Coastal route around Clematon Hill takes coast path off-road. This is the first recorded improvement achieved by the Association.

69 OFF COVE TO STAREHOLE BAY
More coastal route around Bolt Head.

70 SALCOMBE
Originally a coast path route was not provided through the town. An official route is now provided but mainly on roads.

71 STRETE TO STOKE FLEMING
New more coastal route now open. (Central section of proposed improved route from Strete Gate to Warren Point.)

72 WARREN COVE TO DARTMOUTH CASTLE
Coastal route now provided where the authorities

had originally said that the section was unsuitable for a coast path. This was due to the generosity of the Women's Institute that celebrated a jubilee by buying the land and presenting it to the National Trust.

73 KINGSWEAR CASTLE TO MAN SANDS
Original plan favoured by Devon County Council and the then Countryside Commission was to have miles of inland walking on this section. Coastal route now provided on this splendid 6-mile section.

74 BRIXHAM
Originally a coast path route was not provided through the town from Shoalstone Point to Outer Harbour. An official route is now provided mainly on pedestrian promenades.

75 TORBAY
Originally a coast path route was not provided from Goodrington Sands to Torquay (Thatcher Point). An official route is now provided mainly on roads and some promenades.

76 VALLEY OF ROCKS (WHITSAND BEACH) TO MAIDENCOMBE BEACH
Path now provided on coast via Bell Rock.

77 SHALDON TO TEIGNMOUTH PIER
Route through town for coast path now officially recognised

78 HOLCOMBE TO DAWLISH
Path provided closer to the coast but the opportunity to have a really coastal route that eliminated main road crossings was turned down by the then Countryside Commission.

79 DAWLISH WATERFRONT
Originally there was no coast path on this section. An official route is now provided with a bad weather and high tide alternative.

80 DAWLISH WARREN TO STARCROSS
Originally a coast path route was not provided on this section. An official route on roads is now provided.

81 EXMOUTH
Originally a coast path route was not provided through the town from quay to east end of promenade. An official route is now provided.

82 SIDMOUTH
Originally a coast path route was not provided through the town from Jacob's Ladder to the River Sid. An official route is now provided mainly on roads. The route was later enhanced by the opening of the Clifton Walkway seaward of Connaught Gardens.

83 LITTLECOMBE SHOOT TO BRANSCOMBE DOWN
Coast path provided closer to the coast.

84 SEATON
Originally a coast path route was not provided through the town from Seaton Hole to River Axe. An official route is now provided mainly on roads and promenades.

DORSET

85 LYME REGIS
Originally a coast path route was not provided through the town from The Cobb to Charmouth Road. An official route is now provided mainly on roads.

86 BURTON FRESHWATER
Coast path provided closer to the coast.

87 ABBOTSBURY
Path has been taken out of village and south of Chapel Hill.

88 LANGTON HIVE POINT
Path provided on the coast.

89 ISLE OF PORTLAND
Portland's fine 12-mile coast path and links along the causeway now included as part of the National Trail.

90 WEYMOUTH
Originally a coast path route was not provided through the town from Sandsfoot Castle to Overcombe. An official route is now provided mainly on roads and promenades.

91 LULWORTH RANGES
Linking rights of way at each end and the permissive coast path though the MOD ranges now considered as part of the official route.

92 SWANAGE PIER TO NORTH BEACH
Originally a coast path route was not provided through the town from the pier to North Beach. An official route is now provided mainly on roads and promenades

93 STUDLAND VILLAGE
Coast path removed from road through village and on to new coastal route.

South West Coast Path Improvements

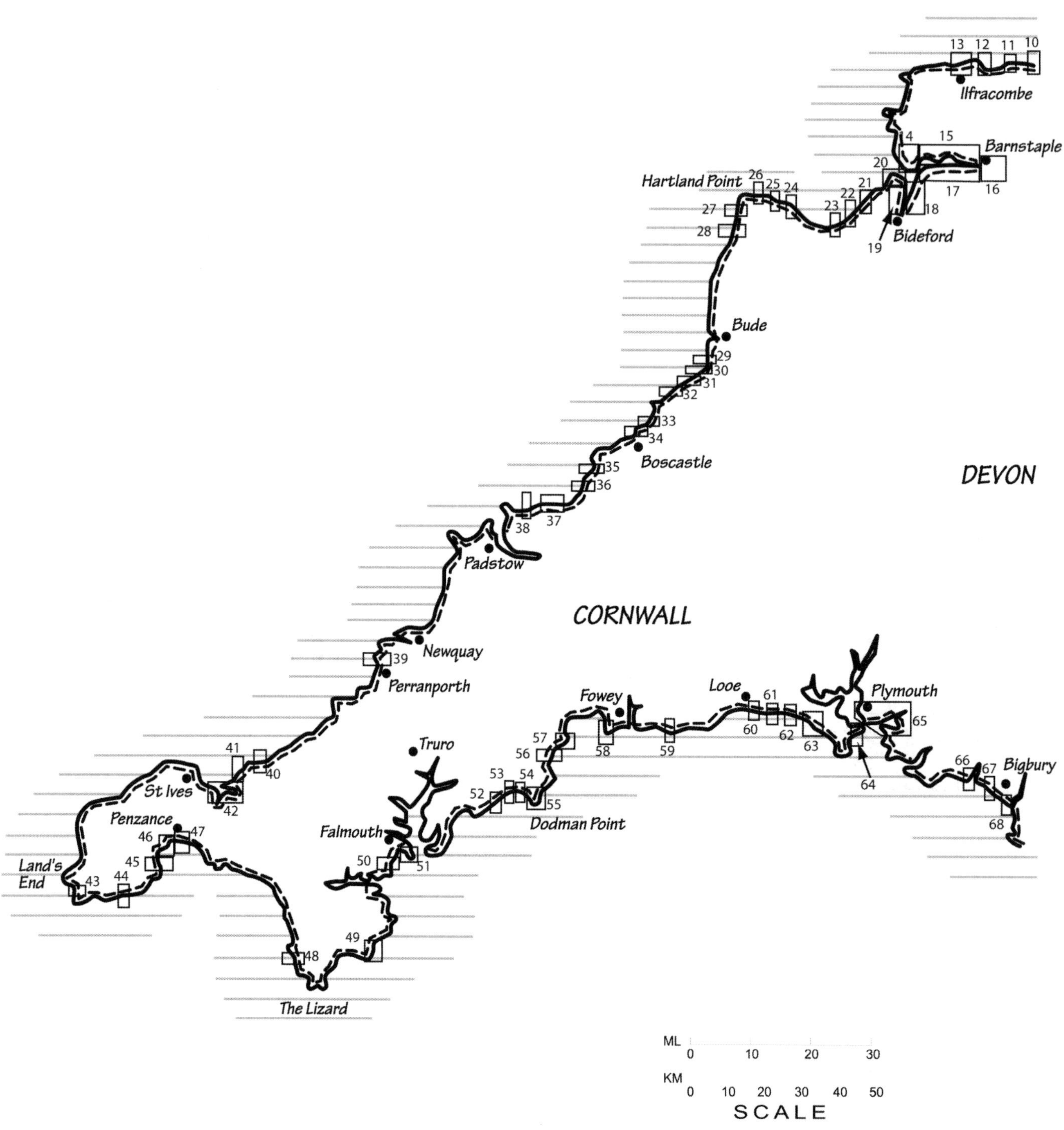

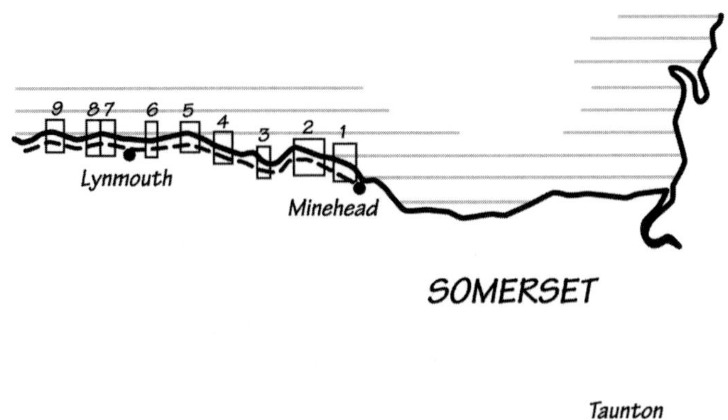
9
8
7
6
5
4
3
2
1
Lynmouth
Minehead
SOMERSET
Taunton

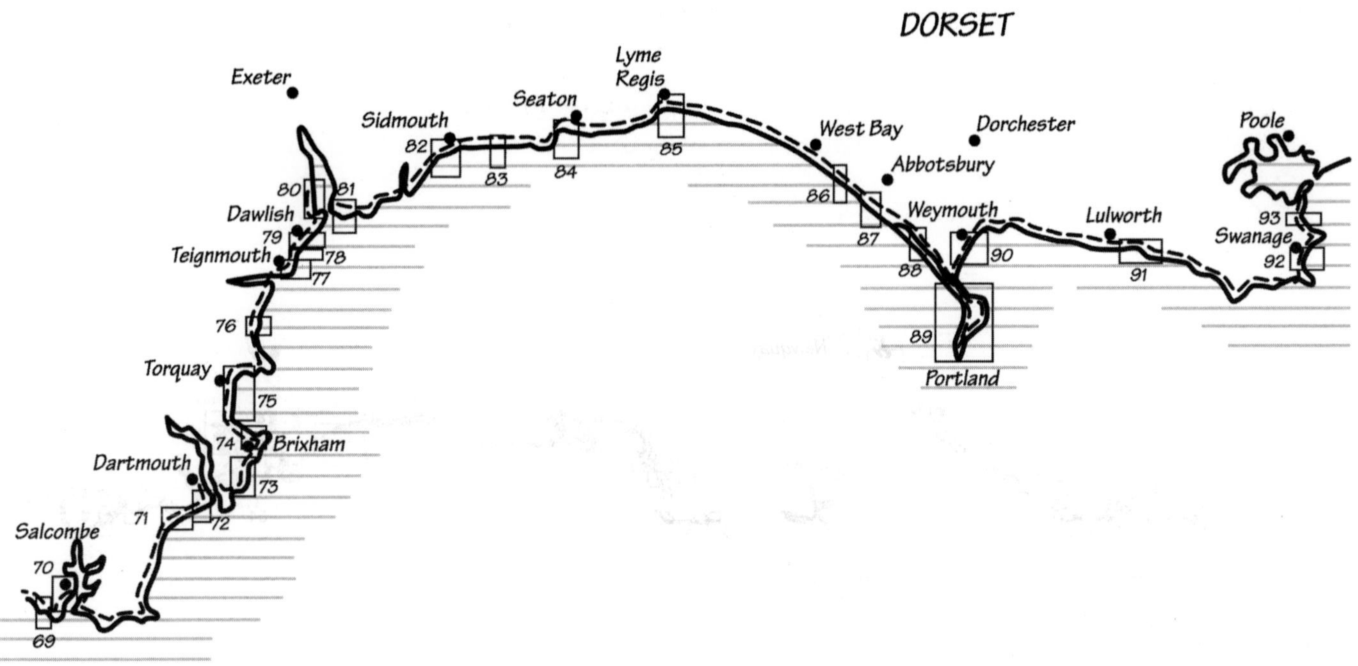
DEVON
DORSET
Exeter
Lyme Regis
Seaton
Sidmouth
West Bay
Dorchester
Abbotsbury
Poole
Weymouth
Lulworth
Swanage
Portland
Dawlish
Teignmouth
Torquay
Brixham
Dartmouth
Salcombe
69
70
71
72
73
74
75
76
77
78
79
80
81
82
83
84
85
86
87
88
89
90
91
92
93

Index

This index tries to tell you briefly who people are or what they did. An attempt has been made to identify similar and remote places by giving additional geographical information. However, it is admitted that if you already know the coast well, they may confuse you! Illustrations are shown in Italics.

Q

R

S

MEMBERSHIP APPLICATION FORM

Please photocopy or phone

Name(s)_ _

Address _

_ _

_ _ _ _ _ _ _ _ _ _ _ _ _ _ _ _ Post Code _ _ _ _ _ _ _ _ _

Telephone _

Email address _

How did you hear of the Association?

_ _

Subscriptions:

If you are renewing your membership please tick here ☐

£11.00 - individuals
£12.50 - joint for couples
£18.50 - Associations / Local Authorities
£16.00 - Non United Kingdom

Life Subscription:

£160.00 - individual, or £185.00 - joint

Payment Details:

Payment made by: ☐ Cheque/Switch

☐ Amex ☐ Visa/Mastercard

Valid from _ _/_ _ _ _ Expiry _ _/_ _ _ _

Last 3 digits on reverse _ _ _ _ _ _ _

Insert card/Switch No. on line below Issue No: ☐

_ _

Signature(s) *Please sign here* Date:

Cheques payable to: South West Coast Path Association

International Money Orders should be drawn on a London Bank.
We cannot accept Eurocheques.

Gift Aid

Under the Gift Aid Scheme the Association can reclaim the income tax paid on any donation or membership subscription received, provided you are a UK taxpayer. If you would like to help us in this way then please indicate below and sign. All that we ask is if you cease to pay income tax in the future, please let us know.

☐ I am a UK taxpayer and would like the South West Coast Path Association to reclaim the tax paid on any subscriptions or donations I make to them.

Signature(s) *Please sign here* Date:

Please send completed form to:

Lizzie Wallis, Administrator
South West Coast Path Association,
Windlestraw, Penquit, Ermington, Devon PL21 0LU
Telephone/Fax: 01752 896237

MEMBERSHIP APPLICATION FORM

Please photocopy or phone

Name(s)_ _

Address _

_ _

_ _ _ _ _ _ _ _ _ _ _ _ _ _ _ _ Post Code _ _ _ _ _ _ _ _ _

Telephone _

Email address _

How did you hear of the Association?

_ _

Subscriptions:

If you are renewing your membership please tick here ☐

£11.00 - individuals
£12.50 - joint for couples
£18.50 - Associations / Local Authorities
£16.00 - Non United Kingdom

Life Subscription:

£160.00 - individual, or £185.00 - joint

Payment Details:

Payment made by: ☐ Cheque/Switch

☐ Amex ☐ Visa/Mastercard

Valid from _ _/_ _ _ _ Expiry _ _/_ _ _ _

Last 3 digits on reverse _ _ _ _ _ _ _

Insert card/Switch No. on line below Issue No: ☐

_ _

Signature(s) *Please sign here* Date:

Cheques payable to: South West Coast Path Association

International Money Orders should be drawn on a London Bank.
We cannot accept Eurocheques.

Gift Aid

Under the Gift Aid Scheme the Association can reclaim the income tax paid on any donation or membership subscription received, provided you are a UK taxpayer. If you would like to help us in this way then please indicate below and sign. All that we ask is if you cease to pay income tax in the future, please let us know.

☐ I am a UK taxpayer and would like the South West Coast Path Association to reclaim the tax paid on any subscriptions or donations I make to them.

Signature(s) *Please sign here* Date:

Please send completed form to:

Lizzie Wallis, Administrator
South West Coast Path Association,
Windlestraw, Penquit, Ermington, Devon PL21 0LU
Telephone/Fax: 01752 896237